The Best
Women's Stage Monologues
# of 2007

The Best
Women's Stage Monologues
of 2007

edited by Lawrence Harbison
foreword by D. L. Lepidus

MONOLOGUE AUDITION SERIES

A SMITH AND KRAUS BOOK

Published by Smith and Kraus, Inc.
177 Lyme Road, Hanover, NH 03755
www.SmithandKraus.com

First Edition: January 2008
10 9 8 7 6 5 4 3 2 1

Cover illustration: *Wardrobe* by Lisa Goldfinger
Design and production by Julia Hill Gignoux

The Monologue Audition Series
ISSN 1067-134X
ISBN 978-1-57525-587-3

Library of Congress Control Number: 2007939332

**NOTE: These monologues are intended to be used for audition and class
study; permission is not required to use the material for those purposes. However, if there is a paid performance of any of the monologues included in
this book, please refer to the Rights and Permissions pages 102–104 to lo-
cate the source that can grant permission for public performance.**

CONTENTS

FOREWORD

In these pages, you will find a rich and varied selection of monologues from recent plays, almost all of which have been published and are thus readily available to you when you have found that perfect monologue to work on in class or to use for auditions. Many are for younger performers (teens through thirties) but there are also some excellent pieces for women in their forties and fifties, and even a few for older performers. Many are comic (laughs), many are dramatic (generally, no laughs). Some are rather short, some are rather long. All represent the best in contemporary playwriting.

Many of the playwrights whose work appears here may be familiar to you — such as Theresa Rebeck, Terrence McNally, A.R. Gurney, Mark St. Germain, Stephen Belber, Lanie Robertson and Lawrence Roman, all of whom have had their work produced On and Off Broadway; but you will also find some exciting new voices, up-and-comers like Anna Ziegler, Kathryn Walat, Rajiv Joseph, Scott C. Sickles, Victoria Stewart, Boo Killebrew, and Andy Chmelko.

After seven years of doing these books for Smith and Kraus, I have decided to step aside and have turned over the reins to my old pal Lawrence Harbison, who knows as much about the theater and its plays and playwrights as anyone I know. It has been a very rewarding and very challenging task editing these anthologies, but now it is time to hang up my red pencil. I am retiring to Myrtle Beach, there to become one of those geezers who stands around all day in a kilt, sending foursomes of awful golfers off the first tee. In my free time I won't be reading plays: I'll be taking up bungee jumping, hang gliding, and allligator wrestling. There is life beyond the theater.

Break a leg.

— D. L. Lepidus, Editor
Myrtle Beach, S.C.

ALL THIS INTIMACY
Rajiv Joseph

Comic
Jen, twenties

> *Jen is trying to communicate with her boyfriend, Ty, who has severe
> laryngitis and can only write his replies to her. So this is a scene, but
> only Jen is actually speaking. Quite a challenge for you!*

(Ty's apartment.)

JEN: Ty . . .

I wasn't going to bring this up today, but seeing as you have laryngitis, I figured this might be the best time to have this conversation.

Because any inclination you might have to interrupt me, well, that just won't be possible because you can't speak. Ha. Oh well.

OK, OK . . . Just sit still for a second and let me speak before you start scribbling away like a madman, jeez! I knew you'd do this or something, just sit and let me say my peace!

(Jen reads what he wrote.)

Look, I know it is, but I kind of have to seize the moment here. Whenever we talk you always talk me out, you put words in my mouth.

(Ty writes again and shows the page. Jen reads.)

No! That's NOT what I mean!

Listen

OK. Ty:

(Beat.)

So. As you know. As we both well know . . . There has never been a time in my life, really *ever,* when I haven't been, you know . . . *in school.* And I know I'm always saying this, OK?

Let me finish!

(Jen reads the notebook. Ty scrawls something brief. She reads.)

You know I don't like that word, and it's rude.

(He scrawls another word, seemingly profane.)

Nice. Thank you. Shut up.

OK! God! I can't believe you have laryngitis and you're still interrupting me! Constantly!

Look, I'm going to talk and you can listen or you can not listen, but here it is. When it comes to figuring out what to do with my life, I've been seriously claustrophobic. Because choosing things narrows down your life, it limits you and it freaks me out. I'm not kidding. Every time you make a decision, you narrow your life more and more . . . I mean that's what you're supposed to do! It's about carving out an identity before you get old and die!

(Ty scrawls.)

No. NO! I don't want sushi! I'm not *staying for dinner!*

(Ty scrawls.)

BREAK UP, OK? BREAK. UP. Me. Break Up. With You. How about that! Oh, but this has never happened to Ty Greene before because he's too smooth a talker and no one can ever get two words in —

(Ty scrawls.)

I'm not going to read your shit!

(Ty writes. Shows her earnestly. She reads it in spite of herself. She looks at him and then away.)

We've talked about this!

And don't look at me like that! You know. You have your book and your job and you're hot shit and all that, so you don't know what I'm talking about.

(Ty scrawls "So?!" and shows her.)

So that's it. And by the way, a year ago you broke up with me. Out of the blue! So don't act all heartbroken.

(Ty looks at her, heartbroken.)

Yeah yeah yeah.

(Ty scrawls something shows her.)

Very funny.

No! I *don't* want that. That's what we've *been* doing. No more fooling around. No more hooking up. No more having your cake and eating it too.

(Ty scrawls.)

That's what I meant by cake.

(Ty scrawls one word.)

It's not you. I just never feel that we're on the same page.

This is what I'm talking about, Ty.

I'm trying to pull things together. I love you, but when I'm around you, things come apart.

They come apart.

ANDROMEDA'S GALAXY
Alan Haehnel

Comic
Ann, teens

> *Ann (Andromeda) has clearly seen way too many* Star Trek *episodes.*
> *In reality, she's driving to school, but in her mind she's on a starship*
> *not unlike the* Enterprise.

ANN: Aah! Out of time and I haven't explained myself yet. Are you understanding at all? How can I make myself clear?

All right, look: This is my brain. This is my brain on *Star Trek*. I was named Andromeda, because of Mrs. Mackafee's day care, because of . . . I really can't say what else — this is how I think. I mean, right now I'm about to park at Langdon High School but, but, but, but . . . this is what has been happening in my mind. I can't help it. I wish it weren't this way. It is though, and I wanted you to know, and if I had more time I, I might find the courage to tell you about the black hole thing and . . . the Brad. We're out of time, though, so at least I told you and now I think you'll be witnessing my destruction shortly but I can take some comfort in knowing that you'll be able to tell your friends, "You know, I once heard of this really strange girl named Andromeda whose entire inner landscape was dominated by a television set from a science fiction series." And I suppose that's good, that I'll live on in that small way after my . . . cancellation.

BABY'S BLUES
Tammy Ryan

Dramatic
Susan, mid-thirties

> *Susan, a first-time mother, is talking to her younger self at age nine,*
> *who is giving her infant daughter a bath.*

SUSAN: I had this weird dream. I dreamt I was taking clothes out of the
washer, and there was something dark and sopping wet at the bot-
tom of the washer, jeans or something, and I had to yank to get them
out, and when I did, it was the baby. Actually two babies and I had
to decide which one was the real baby. They looked exactly the same,
but I knew I had to choose one so I did, and dropped one in the
garbage can, which landed with a thud and didn't move, so I figured
I had chosen the right one. But the baby I kept lay on the changing
table with her eyes closed not moving, so I worried I picked the wrong
one. The changing table changed into a large piece of white paper.
There was a knife lying on the paper. I knew I had to cut her open
and find her tiny organs, to discover how they worked. I had to dis-
sect her in order to know if it was the right baby, so I could take care
of her. She was splayed on the paper like a little frog and I watched
my arm reach for the knife, saw my hand pick it up and push the
knife in, like a surgeon. I heard a little pop and then it slid right in,
but I couldn't find any organs, just blood, blood in the bathtub, and
I couldn't find the baby because she was under the water; all I could
see were my own hands holding her under the water. *(Brief pause.)*
It would be so easy to push her head under the water.

BABY'S BLUES
Tammy Ryan

Dramatic
Susan, mid-thirties

> *Susan is talking on the phone to David, her husband, who has been
> out of town on business, and who has left her alone with their in-
> fant daughter for ten days. She's flipping out.*

SUSAN: Oh, David, oh my god, thank god it's you. I did what you said, I
took her out, for a walk to the library. I was fooled at first, lulled into
thinking everything would be all right. So proud of myself walking
down the street, hey, look at me, I'm pushing a stroller. I'd gotten her
in her snowsuit, and outside, we're going to the library like any other
normal mother and her child. And then I got there. What were you
thinking? *(Beat.)* I took her to the library, like you said, the library
and I swear to god, the janitor, the cleaning guy, he was going to take
us all *hostage.* He'd locked the door, he said by mistake and I never
noticed before he was an Arab I thought he was African American,
but he isn't. And have you noticed there are more of them. They are
on every street corner, talking on cell phones, coming out of apartment buildings, driving by in old Hondas with Massachusetts license
plates, with video cameras, David — the janitor in the library. He's
strange, you have to admit, the way he looks at you, like he knows
you suspect him, like he's *guilty* already. That's the way a *terrorist* looks
and don't tell me I don't know, I saw it in his eyes and I don't trust
him and not with a baby for godsake and I'm standing there, shocked
speechless the door was locked and he had locked it and I'm thinking, I have nothing to feed this baby with, she's going to get hungry
and she's going to start screaming and you know how she is she
doesn't stop until you feed her and I had no *bottle with me,* first of
all what the fuck is wrong with me that I go out for a two-hour walk
with no fucking bottle, not even a goddamn pacifier I deserve *everything* everything I get, I told that doctor and she wouldn't believe me,

she said try the soy as if that was the answer to all my problems well I tried the soy drank it myself in fact and almost threw up it was awful because it's nothing but chemicals, chemical soup, so we won't even get into that conversation since I already told you what kind of half-assed retarded mother I am. *What? What? (Brief pause.)* You don't understand. We live in a Jewish neighborhood. I know we're not Jewish but that's where we live, you can't tell me they don't have a plot to blow up Jewish neighborhoods. Then why do they have policemen everywhere? I might be crazy but I'm not blind. It doesn't matter. They've already won. Because even if they don't commit the act, there are imaginary random acts of terror going on in my brain *every day.* Yes, I think about it every day David, don't you? When you walk on that plane tomorrow, or tomorrow or whenever the hell it is you are coming home I thought you were coming home a year ago, you are coming home tomorrow aren't you? I told you ten days would be too long, it was too long David, too long. I just got pushed over the brink I am hanging on by my fingernails because I love her so much and I know how dangerous it is to have me as her mother — I see you staring at me behind that chair. I don't know if I can survive this David, it is too profound, it is too much painful animal love I had no idea how gut-wrenching this would be. No, there is nobody else here, don't be jealous, I know how I've neglected you these last months, but it's nobody's fault but your own you wouldn't listen like somebody else is listening. Look at her how she has no idea how close she came to not being here today, if that janitor decided to go and do it, her head if you could see it snuggled under my breasts and she's listening to my heartbeat as if I am the world and my breath is the ocean, my voice the stars, my hands the air and she is so trusting that nothing will ever hurt her, and it is a *lie David a big fat lie;* when I see her like this I try to communicate to her how much I love her and that I will try oh god I am so sorry I will try to protect her no matter how I feel about it, I would kill with my nails and teeth the first thing that would come near her including you buddy, including me, especially including me, so come home or don't come home but don't say I didn't warn you, because it is *red alert now David, red alert!*

BFF
Anna Ziegler

Dramatic
Lauren, teens

> *Lauren is telling her BFF (best friend forever) Eliza that she and
> her boyfriend have finally gone "all the way," and what happened
> at school when he blabbed about it.*

LAUREN: Yeah. So. It was two nights ago. We were going to wait for the
end of the school year but, well, Jason really wanted to and I figured
what's the difference between now and June, right? *(Beat.)* But I mean,
well, we were in his brother's room . . . and the walls in there are brown
and it's dark and it smells kind of like gym socks and some weird
cologne. And then . . . afterwards there were no candles and Jason
didn't say much . . . No! I mean, it was *great*. It's just that, I mean, I
figured . . . it would feel more different than this, not being something anymore. But really I'm just still . . . whatever I was. *(Beat.)*
And then Julie found out about it, and I told her it was none of her
business. But she said she heard it from a "confirmed" source and
when I started walking away she said "Jason, Jason told me" and I
turned around and slapped her. I don't know what came over me.

> *(Beat. She waits for Eliza to speak, but she doesn't.)*

Anyway she looked so shocked. SO shocked. Like she'd just fallen
down ten flights of stairs but had survived . . . But then she told me
she'd slept with Jason too, before me. She told me they still hung out
sometimes, which I think was supposed to mean that she still sleeps
with him. She said she convinced him to go out with me because I
needed some male attention. She said a lot of things . . . so I spat on
her shoes. Her new shoes . . . and she kicked me. See?

BLASTER
Victoria Stewart

Seriocomic
Cynthia, teens. Different and not afraid of being so.

Cynthia is giving a lecture in defense of computer hackers.

CYNTHIA: *(With a smirk:)* "The first rule of Fight Club is, you do not talk about Fight Club." But since I want a good grade and everything I say can be found on the Web, I think I'm safe.

The term *hacker* at first just referred to someone with mastery in computers. At MIT in the 50s and 60s, hackers figured out the phone system and railroad switches. They were celebrated for their work and had the support of major universities. In 1969, a blind college student, Joe Engrassia, realized he could whistle a perfect 2600 cycle tone into a phone line and get free long distance. *Phreaking,* the term for hacking into the telephone system, was born.

In 1971, the Homebrew Computer Club published an article about how to build "Blue Boxes" that could make that tone so that anyone could "phreak" if they wanted. This, by the way, was illegal. These Homebrew guys wanted everyone to have access to computers, because up until then, only universities and the military had them. Two of these guys, Steve Wozniak and Steve Jobs, started Apple Computers and Bill Gates built Microsoft and yeah, surprise, surprise, once they started making money, it was all about the "rights of ownership" rather than the free access of information that they were all about when they started.

In the 1980s, suddenly, there started to be a lot of laws against hacking, including going into a system without the "authority" to do so, even if you didn't break anything.

(She stops reading off her cards and looks at the audience.)

Let me tell you something.

Most hackers are not trying to "bring down the system." Most hackers just want to see how things work. They just want to *explore.*

Here's a quaint, 1950's way to look at it. In the old days, kids would break into the old abandoned house at the end of the block.

Maybe you just wanted some privacy, a place to be, alone and away from the expectations of your parents.

Or maybe it was the closest thing to being someplace new. What's inside? How do other people live? And as long as you didn't break or steal anything, you'd get a slap on the wrist.

That's what we're doing. We're just tip-toeing through Boo Radley's house.

So leave us alone.

Thank you.

BLOOD ORANGE
David Wiener

Dramatic
The Girl, fourteen, pretty but with a bad dye job

The Girl tells her friend Clinton about when she freaked out during her first visit to the gynecologist.

THE GIRL: It's some kind of ceremony and there's people. My mom's in the crowd. She looks all scared. And in the middle — it's like this big ring — like a what-do-you-call-it — like arena, and I'm getting led in by these big nameless-faceless guys. And there's this table. One of those nameless tables. Medical table. With the things for your legs. And they put me up there and strap me in. I got a white robe on. They strap me in and spread me. There's this doctor type guy. He's got a mask, you know. Like they have. And all of a sudden I get it. Like I thought it was fun or something before. Like it was a show. But it's not. He's got this thing. Like a long, white thing with a handle and like a light on the end. He's gonna check me. And he checks me and turns around and all the lights change and get all red and everybody gasps. All upset. My mom's all upset. Crying. And I'm crying. And the white thing. The checking thing starts growing in his hand, getting long and sharp. he walks towards me. I start screaming. I'm screaming that it happened riding horses. I'm screaming gymnastics. He shakes his head. Everybody knows it's a lie. I see you. I want you to tell them. I want you to stop them. I want you to say I didn't do it myself. I want you to save me. I'm screaming for you to save me. But you don't hear. Or you do and you just . . . I don't know.

THE BLOWIN' OF BAILE GALL
Ronan Noone

Dramatic
Molly, late thirties, Irish

> *Molly is a painter, working on renovations of a house owned by an English couple. Here, she is talking to Laurence, an African man recently hired as a laborer, whom she calls "Lionel."*

MOLLY: Eamon's mother — and it was her family descended from rent collectors during that famine — not liked, well, she opened a shop one day in direct competition to old Mr. Carson, and having sold all her eggs in one day, went over to old Carson's shop and asked him for six eggs. He told her she could beg and he still wouldn't even give her a drip from his nose. And he laughed at her. That's the type of jealousy ya'd come against here. And then revenge. You know what revenge is?

. . . Well, it's a greater conviction than any other in this town, and ya hold it like your breath so that ya never breathe properly until ya get that person back that insulted ya or laughed at ya. Eamon's mother, Mrs. Collins, stopped breathin' properly. And you could hear her whisperin' to herself, "Six eggs, six bloody eggs. Ara, ara, ara." *(Defiant in telling a story imbedded in her also.)* Then there was my mother, an unusual type, came from stock that never carried animosity, helped a shot English soldier once, charitable, way back in the War of Independence. Well, she tried to help them make peace. *(Pause.)* But the day my mother died, Mrs. Collins jumped up sudden from my mother's bedside and went straight over to old Mr. Carson's shop. "What do you want," said old Mr. Carson. "Mrs. Black says she would like to pay her big bill." Fifty pounds and five shillings, and about time," he said. "Well," says Mrs. Collins, "she died fifteen minutes ago, and you might as well write that down as bad debt. I just wanted to see someone get ya in the end." And she laughed at him. Five years later, old Mr. Carson sold his shop, purposely, to a big conglomerate. Super price. They extended the premises and supplied the village with all its needs, and Eamon's mother lost her business because of it. And the day they closed, old Mr. Carson came over and says, "Well, Mrs. Collins, I wonder who got who in the end now." And he laughed at her.

. . . Loud as thunder, Mrs. Collins died soon after, they says it was a heart attack but most agree it was a buildup of bile that killed her. Their only son, Eamon Collins Jr., was sent to his cousins the Toners to live. Old Mr. Carson died within the year as well, some say coz he had no other objective than to outdo Mrs. Collins and that was done. His older son drank himself to death with the proceeds of the will, and one the day of that funeral we waved good-bye to the younger brother, the GC, who had no choice but to emigrate to America. And that's the "some things" Eamon can't let go of. Does that make sense to you, Lionel?

CAROL MULRONEY
Stephen Belber

Dramatic
Carol, thirty-two

Carol works in a store and paints in her spare time. In this play, she is up on her roof, looking to make connections with those to whom she is closest, and thinking about jumping. This monologue opens the play, and it is direct address to the audience.

CAROL: There are two things about a roof that knock me out. The first is the view. I stand up there, up here, at night, and I look at the sparkling lights down below and I feel like I can figure it all out. I feel like the shock of the city and the traffic and the people — all that stuff that slams you in the face when you get too close — that it somehow becomes beautiful. Uncompromisingly beautiful. *(Pause.)* Because when I go down there, when I come down from the roof to buy a box of . . . eggs — it's like I suddenly have no idea. The whole thing becomes . . . untamed. I go to the store and all I see are the lightbulbs, stripped of their uncompromisingly beautiful sparkle. And I feel like I can't figure anything out.

The other thing about a roof that knocks me out is its edge. Because it scares the shit out of me. I don't like to go near a roof's edge because — I guess this is pretty typical — because I feel like I have the potential to jump. *Is* that typical? I don't know. Part of me knows it is, that it's not uncommon for human beings to have the urge to . . . fall away. *(Pause.)* And the reason it freaks me out so much is because I don't like having that urge. It's not my natural instinct. My natural instinct, I think, is to connect with people. On a very simple level. To feel that what I want and need in life is somehow aligned with what other people want and need, aligned in such a way that we can all, could all . . . live together happily. *(Pause.)* And believe me, I'm not one of these people who says no to everything, or who

14

would jump. Because I wouldn't. In fact, I've tended to say yes more than is good for me, but . . . but it never seems to work out, for me, this desire for alignment. And consequently, as much as I love a roof, whenever I get too near its edge . . . I get that urge.

CAROL MULRONEY
Stephen Belber

Dramatic
Joan, thirty-nine

> *Joan is a friend of Carol Mulroney's, here talking to the audience about her feelings about Carol's death.*

JOAN: *(Beat.)* Carol just wanted to be an anonymous part of the game; to sit at the cafe and smile at all the happy people. To find a way in. *(Pause.)* She wasn't the screwed up one. We are. *(Pause.)* The ones who wanted her to go away, or at least disappear once and for all so that we could get on with our little . . . "plans." *We're* the screwed up ones. The betrayers. It's us. *(Beat.)* The thing is, now that Carol's gone I wanna rip apart the plans. I wanna rip my face off and get at its base; I wanna burn to a crisp the raw membrane of jello-flesh that coats my cracked face — so that the flames rip my thoughts and erase everything I've ever imagined, to the point where I am nothing but a pyre of ashes over which what's left of me can stand and say, "There is Joan, she of big heart and dilapidated liver, there lies her conscience and vigor and faith and guilt . . . there is Joan." And then I want me, my soul, I guess, I want me to lift my foot and stamp myself out, stamp my self to smithereens. Joan wiping out Joan. Joan obliterating this hateful, hurtful, prideless bitch, so that my cunt, my literal and metahypothetical cunt is reduced to dust, to cunt dust, to . . . to . . . to fucking cunt rubble, to cunt *spores* floating gently out to sea. *(Beat.)* And then I want a sailor in that sea, a Turkish merchant marine who's contemplating suicide by stuffing his head into the mechanized ship . . . rudder? . . . I want this sad Turkish boy named *Gobby* to unwittingly intercept my cunt spore, to have it land thoughtfully on his Turkish tongue . . . and to swallow it, and then . . . I don't know what then . . . to live with me, unproblematically, I suppose; to co-exist. To love me, if you really want to know. To love me . . . by having inhaled me. *(Beat.)* But the whole time this is happening — and this is the point — I think — the whole time I'm being cunt-spored away, I want Carol to be watching it all from above; sitting at the cafe . . . and smiling.

CONVERGENCE
Bryn Manion

Dramatic
Cassie, late twenties — early thirties

Cassie is speaking to man in a letter she is composing to him.

CASSIE: I wonder what has become of you. I wonder how my memory would stand up alongside the living version of you. I wonder how long it would take you to recognize me. I wonder if we would pass by each other and never know it. I wonder if we already have. These unfinished letters are a way to cut through the loneliness. To overcome Kibera which is not at all a lonely place. Is it not dissonant to feel the most alone when you are surrounded by nothing but people? This all, all of it, sounds so formal. I hate to think about you, of all people, formally. Which is to say even the thought of you makes me feel safe. We can, both of us, pinpoint the moment when it stopped being safe, when life informed us we weren't the only ones on the planet. But the time before. That was lovely. So perhaps it's not you but a confident, happy, innocent version of myself that I miss. Perhaps that's who you are to me. Perhaps that is what this perpetual, habitual letter is all about? Perhaps.

THE DEAD GUY
Eric Coble

Comic
Gina, thirties to forties

> *Gina is producing what might just be the ultimate reality TV show,
> and she needs a contestant willing to spend a million dollars in one
> week. The catch is, at the end of the week he's killed. She thinks Eldon,
> a young man she's met in a bar, might be the perfect choice, and
> here she's trying to sell him on this great opportunity.*

GINA: A group of contestants have to try to tame wild animals every week.
Alligators, pythons, leopards — the winner gets a million and a new
pet.
   . . . Stitches. Mechanical legs. It's not working out like we'd
hoped.
   . . . But not because of the injuries. Because of the ratings. We're
tanking on Monday nights. That's why I need you.
   . . . No leopards. Totally new show. The network's pulled the plug
on *Heavy Petting* and I promised them I'd come up with something
to fill the last week. To be perfectly honest with you Eldon, it's that
or I'm out on my ass.
   . . . And that's why I need Eldon Phelps. Reality TV is on its
last legs, Eldon, it's wheezing and stumbling around blind, groping
for any lifeline. It's time for you and me to send two million volts
through its rotting flesh, my friend. On our show . . . we get to see
how a totally ordinary, average nice guy who's never caught a break
spends a million dollars —
   . . . Seven days.
   . . . That's the hook of the show! At the end of the week . . . you
die. *(Beat.)*
   . . . Except that it's real. You need to understand that. At the end
of the week you will be legally obligated to truly, really die.
   . . . Hear me out, Eldon, hear me out. I picked a spot on the

map where I thought I'd find people having a hard time. Where I'd find — for want of a better word — losers. And I mean no offense by that. So I found Leadville. And when I arrived in Leadville yesterday, I started asking around about people in the county perceived, rightly or wrongly, as "losers." And your name came up. A lot. *(Eldon starts to speak.)* Which I don't agree with. Not at all. I'll tell you who the losers are, Eldon. It's the jealous, narrow-minded beetleheads who can't see who you really are, Eldon. And I am thanking God that I'm here to open their eyes. You have the personality, the charisma, the charm . . . and I have the money. Together we can blow this whole town — this whole country — wide open. BUT. The only way I can give you this money is if I get the ratings. And the only way I can get the ratings is to have something at stake, something never seen on any television. And that's a man who knows he only has seven days to live, but wants to go out with the biggest party, the most tears — someone about whom the world will say, "Damn, man, he was one of the greats, he had it goin' on! The world's a better place because of Eldon Phelps!"

. . . And I chose you, Eldon. Because, let's be honest, you're already at a dead end, am I right? In your heart, in your gut, you know it is not going to get any better than this. You can either drag yourself from day to day to day like the living dead for the rest of your meaningless life, leaving nothing behind but bad memories . . . or you can go out like a supernova, shining light to lead the world to a better, brighter tomorrow. And have one hell of a time doing it.

DEDICATION; OR, THE STUFF OF DREAMS

Terrence McNally

Dramatic
Mrs. Willard, sixties to seventies

> *All her wealth can't save Mrs. Willard from the cancer that is killing her. It might, however, be able to save a struggling children's theater company. Problem is, Mrs. Willard hates the theater! Here, she is talking to Lou, who runs the company.*

MRS. WILLARD: Lift me to the stage. I can't hop onto it like the young people. I never could. That's not true either. I never wanted to. I detest people who hop up onto things. . . . Much better. See? I can be nice. Now go. . . . I'm in a curious mood today. I woke up in one. I had a good night's sleep, too. There is no pain, and what anxiety I feel is generalized, rather than specific. Oh, I still know I am going to die with and of this hideous disease, but not in the next five minutes. For the next five minutes I am mentally and emotionally cancer-free. I should feel wonderful. I should feel happy. No, this mood is something else. This mood is more subtle, more dangerous. It's taking me within myself. I do not wish to be within myself. This is my question: Why does goodness come so easily to some people and to others not at all? It should be so easy to be good. To be kind, to be generous. Here is the shirt off my back, take it. My heart is yours, it opens itself to you. Goodness should be like breathing: in, out; in, out. Goodness, grace, love. These are the things that should flow ceaselessly from each of us to the other. And so what cosmic life force impedes it? There must be goodness here, in this decaying body, there must be. I would tear my flesh open to find it. I can imagine goodness but I cannot embody it. I can act goodness, pretend it. That's easy for the rich. I write very large checks, even while muttering imprecations against the beneficiaries of my generosity. I detest you,

Goodwill Industries, to the tune of ten million dollars. Die, Starving Children, here's twenty million more; suffer, Incurable Diseases and Everyone with a Disability. Take my money and leave me the hell alone.

EL PASO BLUES
Octavio Solis

Seriocomic
Sylvie, twenties to thirties

> *Sylvie has shown up unexpectedly at the home of Jefe, whom she has never met, claiming to be married to his son Alejandro. What does she want?*

SYLVIE: Ain't Alejandro your hijo? Am I not wedded to him by the El Paso Municipal Court an' before the sight a God? Then I guess I am yer daughter-in-law. An' you are my daddy, Daddy. Mind if I smoke?
(She takes her car lighter out of her purse.)
. . . *(Tossing it.)* Don't work anyhow. Jesus, I'm parched. You got any juice in them cabinets, Daddy? *(No response.)* How 'bout some a home brew? *(No response.)* Just nod if there's a minimart on the corner. *(No response.)* Ah, you're all the same. Tight-lipped old farts. You should see my father. Tight-lipped old fart just like you. I gotta picture of him somewhere in here. He don't look much like he usta. His hair is parted different. Oh, lookie. *(She gets her glasses.)* Muh peepers. *(She puts them on.)* Oh my my my. I was blind but now I see. What a stinkin' rat's ass shithole you call a home, Pops. A bonafide eyesore. Horsefly heaven. Are those stains on the wallpaper or do roaches really grow that big?
(She throws her shoe at tit. Roach goes splat.)
Yep, I guess they do. *(Laughs.)* Sorry, I know them cucarachas are central to your culture. *(Horse laugh.)* Bet your son didn't tell you I was a real card, huh? An' you thought you were just gettin' a beauty.
. . . Lissen, *abuelito.* I'm freein' you of yer obligation. I'll arrange mah own bed an' board, thank you. I ain't this hard up.
. . . My name is Sylvie. Didn't your boy tell you that or was he a little pressed for time? My friends call me Sylvie. An' I ain't drunk. Watch this. I can touch muh nose. *(She stands, spreads her arms apart, and closes her eyes. She stays in this stance during the following.)* None

a this makes sense. None of it. We're watchin' TV over nuts and whiskey an' I step out to the Liquor Barn for ten minutes an' when I come back, Al's ripped off some store an' the police are runnin' him in. He don't explain nothin', he just gives me a kiss and some conditioner an' here I am, with a man I don't hardly know in a house I don't hardly like. I don't fit in my jeans no more an' I got blotches on my skin an' my husband's in La Tuna Penitentiary an' ain't no spirit in my trees. Does any a that make sense to you? *(Slowly, she brings her hands to her face and weeps.)* My man is gone. My Tejano. Only man who ever knew the unfiltered Sylvie Townsend. Gawddamn his sorry ass, I love him. I love my Alejandro. I hurt fer nothin' in this world like I hurt fer him!

FIRST BAPTIST OF IVY GAP
Ron Osborne

Seriocomic
Edith, forty

> *Edith is the indomitable, take-charge wife of a Baptist pastor. Here she is talking to Mae Ellen, a somewhat rebellious young woman who is her church's organist.*

EDITH: Maybe you would've gone on to a wonderful career — in music or advertising alone in a big city — dying to come home to Ivy Gap — to the folks who love you to pieces — but be too embarrassed. *(Beat.)* Being selfish is against my religion, sweetie. Still I'll be grateful to my dying day you stayed put. Who else on the face of God's good earth could've brightened my life like you have for the past thirty years? *(Beat.)* If it helps, Mae Ellen, I've had a few what-ifs myself. I wouldn't trade Charlie for the world. Still, it hasn't been easy having a Bible-toting pastor for a husband. No matter what anybody thinks — including him — I've never bought into the idea we have to walk around with gags in our mouths, spewing chapter and verse. That's why you've been so good for me, sweetie — you never did that. Truth is, you've done things I would've loved to have done — so I haven't needed to. See? On top of brightening almost every single day of my life, you saved me from being tarred and feathered and chased out of Ivy Gap. *(A brief silence as Edith looks at Mae Ellen; she smiles sadly.)* You've even saved me from my biggest what-if . . . if they had chased me away, would Charlie have come after me? Oh, listen to me carry-on. To show you how special you are, I'm going to do something good old Charlie would have a hissy fit over. Still — if you think this little ditty is fitting for our hundredth anniversary celebration — we'll sing it from the top of Ole Smoky . . . *(Sings these words to the hymn "Onward Christian Soldiers" with gusto.)*
>> Onward Ivy Gap
>> Into the next 100 years.
>> With the flag of Baptists
>> Waving in our ears.

GOING TO THE CHAPEL
Donald Steele

Dramatic
Jan, thirties to forties

Jan, who's been married to the same man for several years, is speaking to her friend Julie, who's been married four times.

JAN: I know you've gotten married four times. But I don't know how much of marriage you've experienced.

. . . You've gotten married four times. Had four weddings. But it seems to me when it got rough or hard or not so inspiring or the sex got ho hum and it wasn't so romantic or what it had been at the beginning and it kind of turned from romance into routine, you lost interest in what marriage actually is. It's the romance of the routine. It's an appreciation of the sameness.

. . . you're the reason I stay married. Well, one of the reasons. But on those days, and there are those days, when I look across the table at Dave or I'm sitting on the sofa in my spot and Dave is sitting in his chair in his spot and we're watching whatever it is we watch on this night and that night and maybe the kids are sitting with us, or they're in their rooms doing homework or out with some friends, and I'm thinking "This is my life?," I think of you out there trying to get something started again with someone new and I have a little thrill and some envy because it's like you're on another voyage of discovery and that person is like another country you've never been to and other than Canada I've never traveled and even that was only over to the Canadian side to see the Falls from that angle, I do a little bit of me really does wish I was in your shoes. Especially if we're watching a rerun of something that wasn't that good to begin with. That's how I feel sometimes. I'm living a rerun.

. . . But then I think "Oh thank God I'm sitting on my sofa and he's sitting in his chair just like last night and last week and last month and last year." Not that we don't ever go out. We do. But it's like I've landed. I took my trip. And I'm anchored. And I don't know how I'd do going from port to port. And some times when I think my life is boring, I think of your life and I think I don't have it too bad. 'Cause all that starting over has to be boring too.

. . . I do know I'm grateful to you at those times. Those times when I think "Oh God it's Thursday again."

. . . OK. There is a but. Maybe there is a part of me that is rooting against you. I never thought so. I'm always happy when you ask me to stand up for you. I've never said no. But maybe there is a little part of me that hopes against the hope that I have for you that this is the one, this is the time, this is the marriage that'll work 'cause your life makes my life look full and successful and good in comparison on those days when I think I'd love to be the one opening the door and saying, "Hi there stranger. Come on in."

HOME FRONT
Greg Owens

Dramatic
Jo, fifty

> *Jo is a conservative college professor of business. Here, she is talking to a bandaged woman whom Jo assumes to be an American soldier named "Lucy" who has been placed mistakenly with Jo's family by a mysterious government agency called "Central Security," following a secret military experiment that went wrong.*

LUCY: I wish you'd say something, Lucy. I can't even tell if you're understanding a word I say. *(Beat.)* I made a few calls on my lunch break trying to track down your parents. No luck so far. There are a lot of Smiths. But I have a couple of leads. We'll find them for you, dear. You needn't worry. It would be easier though if you could give me some information. Their first names or where you're from. *(No reaction.)* I always wanted a daughter, you know. I love my Ronnie. Don't get me wrong. He's absolutely perfect in every way. But I always thought it would be nice to have a little girl. Someone I could buy pretty dresses for and put ribbons in her hair. Did you like pretty dresses when you were a little girl? *(No reaction.)* Darwin didn't want another child. I don't know why. He'd never really say. Oh, he'd make excuses. It would cost too much. We'd have to get a bigger house. But I don't think that was it really. I think it had something to do with his experiences in the war. He's never really talked about it, but I know that he was quite troubled for a long time after he came home. That was before I knew him. But even after we were married, he used to have nightmares sometimes. Wake up screaming awful things and crying. Like you. *(No reaction.)* He was terrified when Ronnie was born. I mean he loved him. He's always loved him. In his way. And I know he's proud of him. But I think something about fatherhood really frightened him. The vulnerability. I don't think he could've gone through it a second time. *(Beat.)* I'm sure your parents must be extremely proud of you. What you've done for your country. You're a bona fide hero. Or heroine I guess. That medal on your chest proves it. *(Pause.)* I've sometimes wondered — I'd never say this to Darwin — but I've had my doubts, occasionally, whether this war was really a good thing. *(No reaction.)* I can't tell you how much I admire your courage.

HOW HIS BRIDE CAME TO ABRAHAM
Karen Sunde

Dramatic
Sabra, teens to early twenties

Sabra is a Palestinian woman. She is ferocious but also can be very tender. She has given shelter to a wounded Israeli soldier, her enemy, but after spending the night with him she has strapped on explosives. When he sees them, she is forced to tell him about the massacre of her family and admit that she was born in a refugee camp called Sabra.

SABRA: It wasn't Israelis. You're right. They kept their hands clean. They only opened the gates.

. . . *(She looks at him, drawing into herself, and telling a simple story, with no emotion.)*

I'd gone to the edge of the camp for bread. The babies were crying, hungry again. Angry Timur, just three, and Somaya, who'd sucked Mama dry. I saw Israeli tanks lined up by the fence. The firing didn't scare me much. There was always shooting. I scuttled from shadow to shadow, past sundown now, curfew already, but I got through. I was skinny as a shadow.

On our alley, soldiers were banging at Aruri's, shouting "open up," and that frightened me. I could hear muffled screams down the alley. A man ran past. A shot flashed beside me. He fell, but I wasn't surprised, only wanting to get home fast. Darting, I came to our door, put my hand in the light flowing out. I was glad it cracked open, but about to scold Mama for not barring it tight, when I heard her moan — a deep terrible sound — then I saw. I saw past the soldier's legs to where little Timur was spread on the floor, opened, like a messy fountain, bubbling bright red.

My mouth opened, but nothing came out. A hatchet hung from the soldiers fist. Mama was pressed to the wall clutching Somaya,

I heard her "I swear, this one's a girl." But he tore the baby from Mama, and grunting, hurled her against the wall. "Girls become mothers. Mothers breed sons." Then he brought down his iron-spiked boot, hard on Somaya's face. I shrieked "Mama!" and jumped for his boot in the air, but he whacked me off with his hatchet, and thumped again with his spike, and again, and again, mashing her tiny face. Then he must have been tired, for he twisted back, and swung his hatchet only once more, slicing my Mama's belly straight through. She bent her head forward without a sound. I crawled to her lap. It was a warm long time.

INTELLECTUALS
Scott C. Sickles

Comic
Hera Jane, thirties to forties

> *Hera Jane, a lesbian political activist, is having a drink with Margot, a woman in her forties whose life is in something of a rut. Margot has decided to try being a lesbian. Here, Hera Jane tells her why that's a bad idea.*

HERA JANE: Do you find me attractive?

. . . You just said that I am attractive. In a general sense. What I'm asking is . . . are you attracted to me?

. . . *(Beat.)* OK, Margot, look. I used to believe that every woman, no matter who she was, had a lesbian inside waiting to surface. It was the bond of sisterhood and the innate aesthetic beauty of the female body and the sensitive poetic souls of women that led me to believe this. You know when I changed my mind?

. . . Thirty seconds ago.

There are plenty of women who have revelations late in life. From there, they make tremendous changes. But these women want to be with other women. And, Margot . . . You're not one of them.

. . . If there are two things in this life about which I am certain it's that The Velvet Embrace sucked and you're straight.

This whole "experiment" of yours, Margot . . . It's one thing to experiment with your mind. The mind plays tricks on itself, so it's natural for it to want to play tricks on others. But the heart is sacred. It doesn't know good from bad, right from wrong; it doesn't know anything. It only feels. It only wants, and it wants what it wants because it doesn't know better. It's not always right, but at least it's honest. But when your experiment involves another person's heart, that's when you have to check and see if it's really worth it. Ask your heart what it wants. You'll find out if it's right.

INTELLECTUALS
Scott C. Sickles

Comic
Louisa, twenties

Luisa is married to Nick, but both of them are gay. Here she explains this strange situation to Brighton, who's quite enamored of Nick.

LOUISA: Fast-forward to the summer between junior and senior year of high school.

. . . Nicky's father, the local pastor and pillar of the community, realizes his only son has never had a girlfriend. He goes through hell, high water, and countless Daughters of the American Revolution to find him one. We endure no less than six ice cream socials at which only chocolate and vanilla are served because, and I quote "strawberry is for whores." Ultimately, none of the lovely corn-fed young ladies hold the young man's interest, so he invites Nick to come to one of the meetings he holds at church. In these meetings, men go in "doubting their manhood" and emerge as "good Christians." The pastor says it's "just to observe" — kind of like Take Your Gay Son To Work Day. Naturally, Nicky starts to panic, so I offer to be his girlfriend.

So, one Friday night we stay out really late: until about . . . nine thirty. Can you remember when nine thirty was late? We sneak up onto the porch swing and pretend to shush each other and giggle. We're actually whispering things like "OK, OK, giggle on three. One. Two. Now. Uh-ha-ha-ha-ha! Shhhh!" Finally, we hear someone coming to the door so we, just as we rehearsed, started rubbing noses. Suddenly, Pastor Daldry bursts through the door! We stop rubbing noses and stand up. He looks us over and asks, "What's going on here, Children?" We tell him the truth. "Nuuuthing." The pastor gets this huge grin on his face, pats his son on the shoulder, and from that moment on, Nicky and I are a "couple."

Our parents were so happy! They set the date. They bought the rings. Next thing we knew it was: "I do — I do" — "You may now kiss the bride" — "Everybody do the electric slide" and we were hitched. And that's the story of how I married your boyfriend.

. . . Can you guess where they sent us on our honeymoon?

. . . Colonial Williamsburg. Don't ask me why. Anyway, that night, I was sitting in bed watching gymnastics on cable. Nick comes in, after spending about a year in the bathroom, and starts trying to be romantic with me. I start laughing. He's like, "What's so funny?" and I'm like, "What do you think you're doing?" He says, "Well, it is our wedding night." And I'm like, "Yeah and I'm watching this." And he goes, "Don't you think we should . . ." So I finally come out and say it. "Nick. We're gay." He almost passes out. And I say, "Honestly, Nick. Do you think I'd have married you if we weren't?" And he's like, "You knew?" and I was like, "Hello!"

THE INTELLIGENT DESIGN OF JENNY CHOW
Rolin Jones

Comic
Jennifer Marcus, twenty-two, Asian-American

> *Jennifer is just an average girl who re-engineers obsolete missile components for the U.S. Army from her bedroom. Here, she is in her bedroom, on the Internet e-mailing someone but directly addressing the audience. This is the start of the play.*

JENNIFER MARCUS: *(To the audience.)* Dr. Yakunin says I can trust you. But just because you have a reference like that doesn't mean we're going to work together or that I don't have other options, OK? Let's just say, I've done some research and I know your competition. Ramirez? Bloomstedt? OK? So I'm not going to take a lot of clandestine bullshit, alright? *(We hear a "blip" noise from the computer. To the audience.)* Good. 'Cause I don't want you to think I'm some sort of bitch, OK? I'm not. I'm a lot of fun. OK, so, this is what I know about you. You were a decorated Army Ranger mostly assigned to search-and-rescue missions. You've been a freelance bounty hunter ever since you retired and you work alone. You have citizenship with five different countries under three different names. You have a near 60-percent capture rate which I'm told in your line of work is something close to astonishing and which makes me think, you have some serious low expectations for yourself. OK soooo, you've never been married but you like prostitutes, although you might want to avoid the young ones in the greater D.C. area considering the amount of sperm you donated as an undergrad at Georgetown, OK? *(She hits herself in the head. To the audience.)* Wait, I wasn't supposed to say that. That was my joke to Todd. (Why am I talking about Todd?) I'll tell you about Todd later. That was stupid, 'cause hey, you know, I've had dreams of sleeping with my dad, who hasn't? But they're never sexy and it's fucking gross, you know? OK, weird. I'm a weirdo. Soooo we got off track

35

for a sec, and now we're gonna get back on it. *(She sprays the computer with disinfectant. To the audience.)* I see you've made some creative investments in the last year. Money in Chilean bonds, a racehorse named "El Jefe." In your line of work I guess you just don't have time to master the basics of money management. Laughing out loud!

THE LADY WITH ALL THE ANSWERS
David Rambo

Comic
Eppie, fifties

> *Eppie is the advice columnist Ann Landers. This is a one-woman play. Here, Eppie is responding to a letter asking about the proper way to hang the toilet paper roll in the bathroom.*

EPPIE: *Dear Ann Landers: While I was visiting family back in Sioux City, I brought up the subject of how they all needed to reverse their paper towels and toilet paper on the spools since they were placed incorrectly. The paper should be coming from the wall up toward the top, over and out. They all disagreed. Please settle this for us.*
Signed, "Paper Crazy."

Now, first of all, you come into my home as a guest — relative or not — and tell me how to hang my toilet paper . . . bub, the elevator going down has your name on it.

But be that as it may, I wrote "Paper Crazy" that there was no right or wrong way to hang it, but my preference is the same as his relatives', back against the wall.

And that's how sixty million people found out how Ann Landers hangs her toilet paper. *(Pause. She finds this next statement almost incredible —)* Fifteen thousand letters came in. Fifteen thousand letters! About *toilet paper!*

It just boggles the mind. *(The letter goes back in the file.)* With all the important issues that divide our country — war, morality, abortion, guns, nuclear proliferation — apparently, this is one of the most polarizing issues of the day. Well, let's see if it's still true. *(Directly to the audience, looking for a show of hands.)* Who thinks it should hang down in back, against the wall? How many of you? I'm not asking how it's hung in your house; I'm asking how you *think* it should be hung. Who's for back against the wall? *(She coaxes the response.*

Then — *)* All right. And how many think it should go the other way, come up from behind and hang down in front? *(She coaxes the response.* *Then* — *)* All right. Now, let's see how many of you live in a household where there is disagreement on the issue — the issue of tissue? *(She takes in the response.)* And who's ever gone into someone else's bathroom, taken the roll off the wall, and switched it around? *(To those who respond affirmatively* — *)* Tsk, tsk, tsk . . .

Now, about whether the seat should be left up or down — No, I've got work to do. Besides, the answer to that one's non-negotiable. Right, ladies? *(Back to work* — *)*

THE LADY WITH ALL THE ANSWERS

David Rambo

Seriocomic
Eppie, fifties

> *Eppie is the advice columnist Ann Landers. This is a one-woman play. Here, she talks about how she became "Ann Landers," and about the supposed rivalry between her sister and rival columnist "Dear Abbie."*

EPPIE: I'm not the first Ann Landers. That's an interesting woman named Ruth Crowley, a nurse, and the *Chicago Sun-Times* was running her column. Since I know Will Muneckie, who's an executive at the paper, I call him to see if I can help sort Ann Landers' mail. To keep busy. He says she'd just died very unexpectedly. And they're looking for someone to replace her.

Can you believe that luck? Not her luck — I mean, it's very sad that she died — but that I should just call then.

But I've got a B.S., no M.A., no Ph.D., and I want that J-O-B. So, I use what I *do* have: *chutzpah* and one hell of a Rolodex. *(She does some more bends and stretches.)* The paper gives me some sample letters to answer. One's from a woman whose neighbor's tree drops walnuts into her yard. Legally, whom do they belong to? Well, I don't know the law, so I call an expert: United States Supreme Court Justice William O. Douglas — I know him through Hubert — and then I write what he says the lady can do with her neighbor's nuts.

I answer all the letters like that, by going to the experts. The editor thinks I made it all up. "We'll get sued if we use these people's names!" "But I really know these people," I tell him. "Here are their numbers. Call 'em up." *(Refreshed, she recovers from exercising.)* And that's how I get the job.

Well . . . My column takes off like an Apollo rocket. Papers all over the country pick it up. And the letters just *pour* in.

The job doesn't come with a secretary. So, for a few weeks, Popo lends a hand. Very nice, a helpful visit from a devoted sister . . .

You know the expression, "quick study"?

You have no idea.

Two years later, a *Life* magazine reporter spends half a week with each of us. I must have had rocks in my head to go along with it. And when I see the piece in print, I gag: "Twin Lovelorn Advisers Torn Asunder by Success."

The quotes from Popo . . . ! Honestly, I think sometimes when she puts her mouth in "drive," she leaves her brain in "park."

LARRY AND THE WEREWOLF
Jeff Goode

Dramatic
Spike, twenties to thirties

> *Larry is an unassuming piano player and criminal mastermind.*
> *Spike is a dominatrix lounge singer and double murderer who works*
> *with Larry, and who has much unrequited love for him. Here, she*
> *has reached the end of her rope with him.*

SPIKE: I hope you're happy. *(Before he can react:)* Nuh! Don't even try that
because I'm not gonna fall for it this time.

. . . And don't give me those eyes, Larry, 'cause it won't work. I
got the patch on the other side, and you know I can't see outta this
one. We rehearsed this for weeks, Larry. I worked my ass off for this.
All my life this is what I wanted. This was it. This was our big chance.
I would kill for this. I'd die for this. I'd die and then come back and
kill for this. That's how much I wanted this. That much. Let me fin-
ish. I wanted this for myself, I admit it, but I wanted it for you, too,
Larry. For you and for me. For you and me, Larry, for us. That's who
I wanted this for, Larry, for us. For both of us. For all of us. *(Beat.
She realizes she doesn't want it for Todd.)* Well, for both of us.
Larry . . . you and me . . . we really got something here. Something . . . you know . . . something . . . really . . . unspeakable. No,
that's not the word. Well, you know what I'm trying to say, Larry.
You know 'cause you said it yourself, a million times. . . But I guess
that was just talk, huh, Larry? What is it with you, Larry? Is it drugs?
Gambling? Is it — ? Is it — ? *(She sobs.)* . . . Another woman? *(She
begins sobbing uncontrollably.)* I know I got no dibs on you. I know
you don't care nothin' about me. But Larry, please, I gotta know. Is
that it? If you're gonna rip my heart out, you gotta do it now, Larry,
'cause I can't take any more lies!

LARRY AND THE WEREWOLF
Jeff Goode

Comic
Spike, twenties to thirties

> *Larry is an unassuming piano player and criminal mastermind.*
> *Spike is a dominatrix lounge singer and double murderer who works*
> *with Larry, and who has much unrequited love for him. She thought*
> *Larry was dead; but no, he's not dead.*

SPIKE: Larry! You're alive! Again! Oh, Larry, I'm so glad to see you. Oh, Larry. I missed you so much. When you were lying there dead, all I could think about was so many things. You know all the stuff you never get to say to somebody until it's too late, and then it's too late. . . . It all happened so quick. One minute you were there, and the next minute you were . . . *(She points kinda down at the ground:)* . . . there. I just couldn't believe you were gone. And I guess you weren't gone, so I guess I was right not to believe, wasn't I, Larry? Oh, Larry. I'll never believe you again. I don't mean that the way it came out. I mean the next time you're dead, I won't . . . Well, not that you were dead last time. Obviously. Obviously. Were you? I mean, I saw you shot down in cold blood, Larry. Twice! Didn't I? How could you have survived that? Unless you didn't survive? Or unless . . . Oh, no. Larry, you're not . . . you're not . . . Larry, are you . . . ?
. . . I'm sorry, Larry. I've got so many questions running round in my head right now. Who was that guy? Why did he shoot you? Why did the other guy shoot you? Who was he? What about the record contract? What about Todd? Why doesn't someone shoot Todd? I hate Todd. Why are you looking at me like that? Who are you? What are you? Why are you here? Do you eat red meat? Do I count as red meat? But I know you don't like to talk about these kinda things sometimes, so I'm only gonna ask you one thing. One thing, Larry. *(Pause.)* Can we get married now?

LARRY AND THE WEREWOLF
Jeff Goode

Comic
Spike, twenties to thirties

> *Larry is an unassuming piano player and criminal mastermind.*
> *Spike is a dominatrix lounge singer and double murderer who works*
> *with Larry, and who has much unrequited love for him. She's sup-*
> *posed to be "engaged" to him but the engagement isn't making much*
> *progress and she's had it with his philandering ways.*

SPIKE: Larry?

. . . I'm kinda mad at you, y'know.

. . . You know, it's not the international espionage or the links to organized crime that bothers me the most. And it's not the other women. It's the lying. No, it's the women. No, it's the lying. How can we have a life together if I can't trust you to be honest with me once in awhile? I mean, I got my share of secrets too. You know that. Things I would never tell nobody. But I told *you.* Stuff you know about me could put me away for life. Longer if they make me serve consecutively. But I told you everything, Larry. I got no secrets from you. Of course I guess I gotta trust you, 'cause of how you saved me and all, and I guess I ain't never done nothin' like that for you. But this still ain't no way to treat me, Larry. I'm your wife. Or gonna be. . . . But we all make mistakes. I guess that's the thing, isn't it? You know how awful I been. But you never let that stand between us. You never made me feel like some kinda criminal, just because of . . . well, my criminal record and all. *(Pause.)* Larry, I could forgive you for everything — the other women, and the betraying your country, and lying, and all the other women — if you can promise me one thing . . . No more other women, OK? Can you promise me that, Larry?

. . . Larry . . . I forgive you. That's the way it should be, don'tcha think? Love should be unconditional. . . . Yeah.

. . . You're awful quiet today. *(She takes out a wedding ring.)* I know this wasn't how you planned it. And a lot has happened and . . . Well, we've still got the rings, and I know we don't have a priest, but then you never did believe in God, so . . . Larry Fingers. I love you. Forever and ever and ever. No matter what. See this ring? That's what that means.

LA TEMPESTAD
Larry Loebell

Comic
Iris, twenties

> *This play is an irreverent update of Shakespeare's* The Tempest, *re-set in the present in Puerto Rico. Iris is a young American tourist on vacation with her boyfriend, Sprite, to whom she is speaking.*

IRIS: You can't do this. You have to tell me. This is crucial, Sprite. We have to be able to talk about this. If we can't, it's going to go bad between us. I've been through this with other guys. Everything seems great at first and then there is this "thing," and it's just there but not discussed, and soon it starts to grow and then it's just too big to talk about, and then it's easier to pretend it isn't there and just back away from each other. I don't want you backing away from me, so just say it, OK? Whatever it is. I'm not afraid of anything you can say. But I'd be totally freaked out if I felt there was something you couldn't.

. . . What I want? I want love, friendship, and comfort. I want us to be together forever. I want romance and sex and passion. I want crashing orgasms. I want to be so exciting to you that you throb with desire every time you think of me. I want you to be sitting at your desk at work counting the agonizing minutes until you get to come home to me. I want what every woman wants.

LOOKING
Norm Foster

Comic
Val, forties to early fifties

> Looking *is a comedy about looking for love in a tennis club. Here Val is replying to Nina, another member, who has advised her to set her goals a little lower in the man department.*

VAL: You know, Nina, I happen to think that I'm a pretty good catch.
. . . I'm smart. I have a good sense of humor. I'm well read, well spoken, I've got a good career, and I can look pretty damn sexy with the right outfit and proper lighting. And you know what else? I've got nice hair. Yeah. No split ends, soft to the touch and easy to manage. And with that kind of package you expect me to aim lower? I don't think so, Missy. In fact, if anything, I'm going to aim just as high as I can, because I think I deserve the best. That's right. Somewhere out there is one very nice, very good-looking, very successful man who is going to meet me and say, "Wow. Why aren't you spoken for yet?" And I'll say, "Because I haven't found anyone good enough yet and that includes you, Jerk-off, so hit the road." So, thanks for the advice, Nina, but no, I will not be setting my sights lower anytime soon. In fact, if anything, you should be setting yours a little higher. Like above the waist.

LOOKING
Norm Foster

Seriocomic
Nina, forties to fifties

> Looking *is a comedy about looking for love in a tennis club. Here Nina is talking to Matt, a fellow member and recent lover, about how she's sick of "looking for love in all the wrong places."*

NINA: Look, I'm sorry, Matt, but I just don't feel very good about this right now.

. . . About us. About me. Everything. Dammit. You know, all these years I never thought about this stuff. I went out, had fun, and if I liked the guy, well, I didn't mind sleeping with him. What's the harm, right? Now, all of a sudden I'm second-guessing myself. I mean, maybe I've been wrong all this time. Shit, last month I slept with a married man. Oh sure, I didn't know he was married, but maybe if I hadn't jumped in so quickly. Maybe if I had a more stringent screening process. Right now my screening process is "Have you got a car?" I mean, take you. You recite a stupid poem and boom! We're in bed. I didn't even hear the whole poem! Two lines and I'm naked. God. Why don't I take my time with these things? What's the rush? I'm living my life like it's some sort of sexual relay race and I'm the baton. That's why I don't feel so good about myself right now. Maybe it'll pass. I don't know. But at this moment I'm very angry. In fact, just looking at you makes me angry. You represent everything I don't like about myself. Every man I ever slept with and never heard back from. Every man who ever tried to hit on me with a dumb line or a silly poem. Every man I fell for because I was so damned desperate to have someone love me. You're every one of them. Standing right here in front of me. You make me sick right now!

MADAGASCAR
J. T. Rogers

Dramatic
June, early thirties

*June works as a tour guide of the ruins of Rome. In this, the start
of the play, in direct address to the audience she begins the haunt-
ing story of a mysterious disappearance that has changed her life forever.*

JUNE: People disappear all the time. I don't mean children who are taken
or stolen and then, so often . . . well, we all know enough about that.
I mean people, the over-eighteen kind. Thousands and thousands,
every year. Almost all of them end up being found. Very few are murdered. Comfortingly few. Statistically, less than 2 percent are victims
of "foul play." Which always makes me think of exuberant chickens
running around. *(Beat.)* Or maybe that's just me.

Those who aren't found, nine times out of ten it's because they
chose to go missing. *(Beat.)* I didn't know this. That so many people
choose to step away from their lives. They owe money, someone's preg-
nant, they've done a terrible thing, or they've just had enough. Life
rises and rises, until all you can do is drown or swim away. And if
you haven't broken any laws, this is perfectly legal. Even if you were
tracked down, say, paddling the Congo or wandering alone in the Sa-
hara, no one can force you to go back. If you choose to vanish, you
owe your past nothing.

But what interests me most are those left behind. The ones forced
to go on, never knowing if they said or did something that led to the
vanishing. If they are honest, they will tell you that even when all evidence points to a planned disappearance . . . they will themselves to
reject this, and cling to any alternative they can find . . . even death.

They will tell you that if someone is going to choose to disappear, they need to stay gone. That what is feared most is a return.
Because some do. The tiniest percentage, but they do. Even after years,
they just . . . reappear. As vengefully as they disappeared.

Some things cannot be faced.

MADAGASCAR

J. T. Rogers

Dramatic
June, early thirties

> *June works as a tour guide of the ruins of Rome. Here, in direct address to the audience, she talks about her daily routine in dealing with a mysterious disappearance that has changed her life forever.*

JUNE: Before each tour I have coffee and read the paper here in my room. Someone leaves them outside my door with the mail, on those rare occasions when I have mail. Coffee, paper, tour: I do the same thing every day. The structure gives me something to sink my teeth into. It's important in life to always have something in front of you, that you can focus on and move toward. "Look at your feet," that's one of my rules. "Go forward, keep your eyes in front of you, and *don't . . . look . . . back.*" That's the key. Because when you do . . . for me . . . it's like there's a mountain. Looming. And I stand like a statue, frozen in the shadow of it. *(She points to a blue, worn man's shirt and a pair of trousers.)* I wear the same thing here, every day. Wash it out in the sink, let it dry in the sun. Living here, on my own, it's been amazing to discover what you can do without. *(She gestures to the room around her.)* If you strip away the things that surround you, you learn what you truly need.

This room. It's embarrassing how much it costs. (Not that you can tell, since my "renovation.") Yes, the view from the balcony is lovely; but for the price of living in a hotel these past three years, I could have bought an entire villa. But this was our room. And as my father used to say, "That which we most want, we do. Regardless."

Money isn't an issue for me, of course. Paul would always remind me of that. How lucky we were. Spoiled. Paul wouldn't have to say this. Just a look, and I'd know. Because we knew each other. Down to our bones. Right now, Paul could be sitting in a room — anywhere in the world — he'd know what I was going to say or do next. And why. Everyone needs someone like that. A mirror you can see your reflection in. Making life worth living. *(Beat.)* But living here, I've also discovered the danger in learning new things. Because if you keep digging, one day, you'll discover that something you know in your bones, that defines who you are . . . is a lie.

MAIDEN'S PROGENY
Le Wilhelm

Dramatic
Mary, thirties to forties

> *Mary is the American Impressionist painter Mary Cassatt. She is in
> her studio in Paris, discussing the travesty of justice that was the Drey-
> fus affair with the English critic Wynford Johnston, and her fellow
> painter Edgar Degas' inexplicable silence on the matter.*

MARY: Yes, M. Drefus is a Jew. And it distresses me that an artist as great
as Edgar Degas and that France, the very cradle of modern art, can
be so blind to this injustice. I realize that all of this is now a few years
in history, but still it burns in my very being.

. . . Artists cannot allow themselves to be separated from the
world in which they live, nor, I might add, can critics. Injustice should
be the concern of everyone. And that is what happened to M. Drefus.
He was accused of treason. Found guilty. Then the errors were discovered — egregious errors that would prove him innocent. And what
was done? Nothing? Why? Because he was an Alsatian Jew. It is the
only possible explanation as to why the situation was not rectified.
Emile Zola wrote to the President of the French Republic an open
letter denouncing the cover-up and demanding the release of the pris-
oner. "J'accuse." This letter contained the signatures of over three
thousand people. People such as Manet, Proust, Anatole France, the
Halevys, but it did not contain the signature of Edgar Degas.

. . . I found his behavior brutish and am surprised at your own
support. Everyone in his circle of friends, indeed most everyone of
the educated class realized the travesty of justice, which had occurred.
And all of us did our best by signing petitions and speaking out pub-
licly. But M. Degas remained icy-lipped when the subject arose. I still
see Degas, but our relationship has been forever altered. The whole
affair haunts me.

. . . Yes, you can make excuses. But on something of this

importance, they are unaccepted. He was in the military, fought the communists, one of his eyes was damaged, but how can he not stand for truth? How can he by his silence support an affront against freedom? How can this man who has thrown a glorious light on the most base and ordinary of humanity with no regard to sex or class, how can this man sit icy-lipped and silent as France and her agents persecute and imprison so unjustly? How can he do this? *(She has brought herself to quite a state of agitation and now turns it on Johnston.)* But this does not in anyway lessen the light Degas has shown on humanity. No matter what Degas may or may not be, the light created has its own life, and its beauty cannot be denied!

MAKE ME A MATCH
Lawrence Roman

Seriocomic
Stevie, thirty-eight

> *Stevie, a no-nonsense corporate type, is talking to Robin, a profes-*
> *sional matchmaker whom she has hired to find a mate for her*
> *mother — but the mother won't get married until Stevie does.*

STEVIE: I've heard about sisters feeling that way. The younger one not wanting to get married before the older one does because she loves her
and doesn't want her to feel bad. But of course, if there's a lot of sib-
ling rivalry it could work the opposite. That is, the younger one
couldn't wait to get married before the older one did. Like sticking
her tongue out at her older sister. But with a mother and daughter,
it's not as pressing to the mother. She's been married before. Usually,
that is. Of course, if the mother feels her daughter is getting older
and older and in danger of becoming a crotchety old maid never getting married, then it wouldn't matter much if the mother got married as it seemed the daughter never would. You understand?
    . . . On the other hand, if the daughter is getting older and older,
but still has expectation. That is, her beauty and femininity are coming through. That she is compelling, you know. Well then, a feeling
mother wouldn't want her daughter to feel bad by upstaging her and
getting married even though the daughter as yet didn't have a good
prospect. Understand?
    . . . Of course you do because you figured out my mother's feel-
ings right away. It's true. You do have insight into a woman's mind
being a serial plucker and all . . . Want to go for three?

A MOTHER, A DAUGHTER AND A GUN

Barra Grant

Seriocomic
Beatrice, late fifties to early sixties

Beatrice is talking to her husband, Alvin. Their daughter has locked herself in the bathroom and has a gun.

BEATRICE: You know where I was? I was bringing civilization to the animal world, that's where. You think she was born using a toilet, knowing not to put her hand on the stove, her toes in her mouth? No. These things had to be yelled at her. Every minute. "Don't. Stop. Cut it out." Shlepping, hauling. Wheeling her around in that stroller with the wonky wheels. Looking at people on bicycles. Free people. With good wheels. Biking to God knows where but free to bike.

. . . I'm talking about being out from under, Alvin. Breathing the air. At lunch at that little bistro. With Mrs. Getty. A cultured, civilized group of people who knew where to eat. How to hold a fork.

. . . That was somewhere to be.

. . . Please. You wouldn't know where to begin with Mrs. Getty. Kir Royale. Just the name. Her favorite beverage. All of those women, like they'd walked out of *Vogue*. The hair, the nails. Everything perfect. The way she sipped from that bubbly glass, the ring on her finger like a doorknob. I was alone of course making "to do" lists over an onion soup. She wasn't eating a thing. Kir royales was lunch for her. "Come on over to our table, tell us about yourself." I couldn't believe it. I'd already been eaves-dropping for half an hour. Safaris, Monte Carlo. The places she'd been. Not Miami on half-fare, I'll tell you.

. . . Maybe I hadn't been on a safari but she couldn't get enough of me. "Enlivened." That's what she said. I enlivened the whole table. "Beatrice," she said. "How come we didn't know about you? You're a treasure, a find." She's going to know about me, stuck on 82nd with a view of a wall?

. . . Special, that's what she knew I was. She'd phone me, I'd drop everything. That place of hers. Twelve rooms on Fifth Avenue. Three in help. She never saw her children. Said that's how they did it in Europe. Boarding school. Jessica was five. I asked if they had a boarding school for her. She laughed. "Wishful thinking," she said.

. . . She had a six-year-old. I looked at them together. Jessica, gloomy, clumsy. Her little girl in a three-hundred-dollar playsuit. Bond curls. An angel. "She has her father's features," Mrs. Getty said. "So fine. Refined." I looked at our daughter, I realized she had her father's features too. And she had your way. The way you have of receding into the wallpaper.

. . . I fought to make her different. Be somebody, enliven. Always more like you she became. After I heard the gun in the bathroom I thought, why not? What's the difference? What does she have to live for? Another thirty years of gloom.

A MOTHER'S LOVE
Craig Pospisil

Dramatic
Melissa, thirties to forties

In this direct address to the audience, Melissa tells us why she has done what she has done. It was to save her daughter from all the ills of the world.

MELISSA: Our children need to be protected, don't they? And a parent has to do whatever they can to keep their child from harm. *(Slight pause.)* D-R-U-G-S are everywhere, and I — oh, I'm sorry. My little one is here, so I have to talk in code. Just let me know if I go too fast. Anyway, D-R-U-G-S are everywhere. You see reports all the time in the news. It's going on right inside our schools. *(Slight pause.)* And that's not all. Kids are going to school with G-U-N-S and K-N-I-V-E-S. I don't know about you, but that scares the H-E-double-L out of me. *(Pause.)* I want to keep Theresa safe. She's a little girl, just four years old. Innocent. Kids should be allowed to stay that way as long as possible. They grow up too fast these days. *(Slight pause.)* Life is hard enough. I'm sure we can all agree with that. Childhood should be a time when you don't have all those worries. I want to make sure Theresa has that time. *(Pause.)* I love my husband. Even now, I still love Kevin. Now, he thought it was time to send Theresa to school, and I know he had his reasons. School can be a valuable experience. *(Slight pause.)* But times change. School isn't the same as it was when we were children. My first day of school I was so scared about being separated from my parents and about being surrounded by kids I didn't know. Imagine how much more frightening that would be today, knowing that many of your classmates were A-R-M-E-D? *(Slight pause.)* Now, look, I'm not saying anything would happen while she was in kindergarten . . . of course not. *(Slight pause.)* But after that who knows? *(Slight pause.)* Will Theresa make it to third grade before she starts doing D-R-U-G-S at recess? And after D-R-U-G-S, how long will it be before she's drawn into a world of S-E-X? And S-E-X and D-R-U-G-S lead right to P-R-O-S-T-I-T-U-T-I-O-N. *(Slight pause.)* Did I spell that right? Let's see P-R-O . . . Well, I mean, she could become a H-O-O-K-E-R. *(Pause.)* Not my little girl. *(Pause.)* I tried to convince Kevin we should keep Theresa at home and teach her ourselves. But he didn't understand, and we got into a big F-I-G-H-T. I tried to talk about it in a calm, reasonable way, but Kevin lost his T-E-M-P-E-R and Y-E-L-L-E-D, and that made Theresa cry. I couldn't have let that happen. *(Slight pause.)* Ladies and gentlemen of the jury . . . yes, I K-I-L-L-E-D my husband. But what I did was a form of self-defense. I was protecting my daughter the way any of you would. Theresa's too young to see the world for what it is. She needs to be protected. And this is why I am innocent of M-U-R-D-E-R. *(Pause.)* Thank you. *(Melissa exits as the lights fade.)*

MY DEAH
John Epperson

Comic
Lillie V., old

This farce is a Southern-fried send-up of Medea. *Lillie V. is My
Deah's cantankerous octoroon housekeeper, here talking to some neighbor ladies about My Deah's troubles. She is played by the same actress who plays My Deah.*

LILLIE V.: You cain't see her. She's sick! Oh, Lawsy, if only 'at Ole Miss foot-
ball team hadn't gone on 'at trip to Baton Rouge all 'em years ago!
If only 'at Greyhound bus didn't go right through 'is chere captal o'
Missippi. Then it wouldn't be so dang easy to get down yonder-ways!

If only 'at piece of pine property up 'ere in Yoknapatawpha
hadn't paid for 'em football players to go and try fer 'at gold trophy,
then My Deah wouldn't'a left Baton Rouge. Barely crowned Miss
Loozianner State University — and she run up chere all sexed-up fer
Gator!

If only she hadn't've met him at 'at big party down yonder-ways,
she wouldn't'a left, and broke her mama and daddy's heart.

But, naw, she come on over chere and give him a couple of
young-uns. And she was a good wife. She did all the right thangs.
Got herself 'at big-time job on TV. She made character with all of
you Jackson soci'ty folks and Gator was real happy. I bet he was mo'
happy than any o' yo' men!

Everthang's done gone haywire. It all started goin' wrong when
Gator commenced seein' that head doctor and goin' to night school
I just knows it!

Now he's done found some young gal he wants — name o' Simplicity Bullard, the child of Guv'nor and Mizriz Bullard. You don't
go monkeyin' with them Bullards! And wouldn't choo know Simplicity's done just been crowned Miss Missippi? They say her daddy

bought her the title and maybe 'at's so, 'cause she sho' ain't the purtiest thang you ever laid yo' eyes on!

I guess it's been twenty years since My Deah was Miss LSU. Nobody down 'ere or up here's done ever forgit about it! And 'ey ain't forgotten she left 'ere right after she won it and 'at gal who sang opry took her place!

Simplicity didn't sing no opry in *her* pageant. No, sir! She twirled a baton and wore a fringe bodysuit so the whole thang shook when she twirled. Oh, yes, it was somethin'!

It was trashy, but it was the best thang I seen in 'at pageant for a long time, 'cause that pageant's done gone way down. Waaay down!

MY DEAH
John Epperson

Comic
My Deah, thirties to forties

> *This farce is a Southern-fried send-up of* Medea. *My Deah, a former beauty queen, is on the verge of being dumped by her husband Gator for a pretty young bimbo. Here, she tells some neighbor ladies how she is coping with this misfortune.*

MY DEAH: Mignon, honey, who do you think you're kiddin'? The three of you have always looked down on me all smug and namby-pamby because I work. But I've lived! I've frolicked and I've fucked and I've had fun!

And all you could do was watch. Anyway, I don't care what you think. I just want to lay down and die. Gator was my whole life. And he knows it! Now he's just like all the other men I know — except, of course, all your faithful husbands!

Face it!! Us women are merely junk in this world. Men's lust rules the earth. Can't live without 'em though, so we hook up with one. Don't know: Will he turn out to be good or bad? If he turns out bad, we can't get divorced. That's not respectable. Not here in the polite hospitality of Jackson, Mississippi! And especially not if you are originally from Louisiana, the rival football team of the University of the Goddamn State of Mississippi!

So, you try and make character with people. Try to make nice. Practically have to know witchcraft to make friends, but sooner or later, you do find people to socialize with. Make a good home for your husband, try and figure out what he likes. Want to make him happy — in every way. Even on Sunday!

Maybe you and him are livin' a little beyond your means, but everybody thinks you're a fine couple and they're all envious. Course, he's bound to get restless. And, yes, I know Gator spent quite a bit of time down at that Tiffany's Sho-Bar, but that didn't mean he was lookin' to set up house with any of that trash. So I just bided my time and kept my mouth shut — and made sure my vibrator was workin'!

MY DEAH
John Epperson

Comic
Mignon, forties. Played by a man in the original production

This farce is a Southern-fried send-up of Medea. *Mignon is sort of the leader of the "chorus" of neighbor ladies, here pleading with My Deah not to kill her children.*

MIGNON: The people of New Orleans, sons of The Civil War,
Have enjoyed their prosperity and frivolity since ancient times.
They walked always with grace under the sparkling sky
Because they are children of Hermaphrodite *(pronounced HER-MA-FRO-DIE-TEE).*

They say that kindly he-she
Dips a gilded cup
In the bountiful stream of the mighty Mississippi,
And exhales over the city the breath
Of soothing perfume-laden breezes.

How will such a municipality, welcome
You, the child-murderer
Whose very presence is contamination?

Think about the bloodshed, My Deah.
By your knees, by Nancy Kerrigan's knees!
By Antigone's!
With every plea I entreat you,
Do not slaughter your children!

How will you come face-to-face with their innocence and not shrink back?
You just got to give up this idea . . . My Deah.

'NAMI
Chad Beckim

Dramatic
Keesha, mid to late twenties

Keesha is speaking to an Indonesian orphan baby. She has just learned that the child, whom she has been babysitting under false pretenses, is to be sold to a sex-slavery ring by her husband and her landlord.

KEESHA: How you doin', little one? You good? Pee-yew! Stink like pee in heah. Can't have you smellin' like pee, now, can we? You gonna let me clean you up? C'mere, baby, less get you cleaned up. No? *(Offers the doll.)* You lookin' at this? Iss pretty, huh? You want it? No? You just gonna sit ovah there an stare at me? Thass OK, little girl. Thass OK. You scared, honey? Prolly too tired to be scared, too scared ta be tired. You miss your mother? Your father? *(Long beat.)* I usta wanna know my father — doan remember nuthin' 'bout him 'cept his voice reminded me of smoke. Couldn't begin ta tell you what he look like, juss remember me lyin' in bed an hearin' him talk ta mama, voice like smoke. Fill up a room, then just as quick, be gone. *(Beat; slowly rises.)* I hope thass how my girls remember me. 'Cause I think if I evah woulda found my father, I woulda hated him for what he was. Instead, rememberin' that voice . . . smoke . . . leaves me with one nice thing. Always good ta have one nice thing, I usta have a lil girl juss like you. Two lil girls. Juss like you. They bof with tha state now. Tha first child she got burned in tha bathtub. Tha second one born all sick an twisted from tha rock. Life over for both of those babies before it start. Cause of me. On account of me. I think about them, how they gonna hate me when they old enough ta realize what I did ta them. I have tha conversations in my mind, thinkin' what Ima say when they find me, then hopin' ta God that they have the sense not ta look. *(Long beat.)* I ain't gonna let this happen ta you, lil girl. Ain't gonna let them do this ta you. My husband, he ain't a bad man, juss sorta — sick — or whatevah, but tha other one . . . *(Beat.)* I ain't gonna let these men hurt you . . . and even though I ain't doin' it for this reason, I hope that maybe this will make up for what I done ta my own girls. Maybe not . . . but maybe so.

OFFICE SONATA
Andy Chmelko

Comic
Marisa, late twenties

> *Marisa is an Account Supervisor for her advertising company's Fruity*
> *Fruit Munchies account. She has had it with her slacker assistant*
> *Martin. After he inadvertently humiliates her by replacing her pro-*
> *motional reel with a bizarre pornographic film, horrifying her clients,*
> *Martin is subjected to the company's unique form of punishment:*
> *having to sit there and allow a Termination Alternative Artist (TAA)*
> *to flip him off. Here, Marisa vents her frustrations with Martin while*
> *explaining what's in store for him if he fails to clean up his act. The*
> *TAA has a big fat middle finger in Martin's hapless face.*

MARISA: First offense someone gave him the finger. Second offense two
people gave him the finger. Third offense five people gave him the
finger. The fourth offense resulted in his termination which if I remember correctly went something like this. Fifty people gave him the
finger while they made two phone calls: one to his parents express-
ing the company's disappointment in them for raising him wrong,
and another to his girlfriend to tell her that he'd been seen in a bar
kissing his old high school sweetheart. Then they took turns flicking
his ears, kicking his shins, and urinating in his thermos. Next they
styled his hair in a ridiculously outdated fashion and forced him to
wear a T-shirt that said "Hitler Is My Homeboy." When it came time
for him to leave they shot at him with beanbag bazookas to chase him
to the elevators. Then when he got downstairs two rather large gentlemen grabbed him by the arms, led him out of a special door . . .
and no one's seen him since. You are closely hovering around the two-
finger range, Martin. I suggest you do something about it. You walk
yourself downstairs to that travel agency and don't even *think* about
leaving until you've gotten my discount. Understood?

OVER THE TAVERN
Tom Dudzick

Dramatic
Annie, sixteen

> *Annie is telling her mother how she happened to be seen at a movie*
> *on the League of Decency's banned list.*

ANNIE: The other day . . . me and Tina . . . we sort of took a long lunch
hour at school.

. . . About the length of a movie. Tina said that these two boys
would meet us at the theater. From Bishop Cleary. They take long
lunch hours, too, sometimes. It didn't seem like a great idea, but since
boys haven't exactly been beating down my door . . . Anyway, they
never showed up. They got caught by the school janitor. So, me and
Tina went in. And, this movie, it was sort of . . . artistic. Foreign, actually. I don't think it was on the Legion of Decency list.

. . . But it wasn't dirty! It was beautiful. It really was! And so romantic, I just wanted to die! It took place in this little town in Italy.
And there was this one part where this girl's father forbids her to see
her lover and he locks her in her room. So, that night, while her lover
is outside, she goes to her window and, sort of . . . gets ready for bed.
(She takes a swig of Coke.)

. . . But they didn't show anything. They covered most of it with
trees and stuff . . . and showing his face looking up at her. It was
so . . . artistic! And, so anyway, all day I couldn't stop thinking about
that part. And that night I couldn't sleep 'cause all I could think about
was how she loved him so. And him outside all alone. And then, lying
there in bed, thinking, I just sort of . . . became the girl. I got up out
of bed, and . . . Oh, Mama, I never thought anybody would be watching. I swear! *(Sobs.)*

A PLAGUE OF ANGELS
Mark St. Germain

Dramatic
Mary, thirties

> *Mary is the notorious "Typhoid Mary," a carrier of that dreaded disease who spread it wherever she worked. Here she confesses to the doctor who has identified her as the cause of the epidemic, and she reveals that its first victim was her own daughter.*

MARY: I killed her. I killed them all. *(Mary weeps.)*

. . . On the boat, that's when it came to us, the sickness. all of us, shut up in the dark or crushed like cattle on the freezing deck.

That's where I had her. A new baby for a new land. In the night, in the cold, with all of them staring, standing around me, barely enough room to lay down on the planks. the women waited, crouching 'til she came. And I squeezed my husband's hand so hard I thought he'd scream. But it was her scream I heard, and I thanked God for it. How was I to know she'd be born with it, sick like all of them. I held her in my arms, she was so beautiful. I held her 'til the end, then even still; they had to take her from me.

And himself; with barely the strength to stand. He'd only lived to see her. He took her in his hands, looking down at her like a treasure, watching close, for a breath, but she had none.

He took step after step, slowly, to the rail of the ship.

He looked at me then, then at her, and the water. He wouldn't let her go alone. He dropped over the side, with our daughter in his arms and the waves took them both.

I should have run to them, gone with them then. What was left but the sickness?

POST MORTEM
A. R. Gurney

Comic
Betsy, early twenties

> *Betsy is a college student and head of the Lecture Committee, in-*
> *troducing a pair of scholars who have reconstructed a lost and most*
> *controversial play by a completely forgotten playwright of many years*
> *ago named "A.R. Gurney"; but she goes off on a tangent as a result*
> *of having to start out with the "cell-phone speech."*

BETSY: *(To audience.)* Hi! . . . Welcome to the Marvin and Mona Spell-
berg Memorial Auditorium. My name is Betsy Baker, and I'm this
year's chairperson of our new Student Lecture Committee . . . *(Glances
offstage.)* Oh, and I'm *so* excited! Tonight, right here, on this stage,
I'll be interviewing two of the most important people in the world!
And what's so amazing, they actually met here, not so long ago! One
was a lecturer on drama, and one was her student, and now they're
married, and famous, and they've come back to home base to share
their experiences with all of us! *(Indicating her cards.)* Naturally there
has been so much interest in their visit that we've asked people to sub-
mit their questions ahead of time. And we've tried to select the most
appropriate ones. And here they are. *(Puts cards carefully on the table.)*
O K, but before I introduce our guests, I have to make the usual
speech about cell phones. Namely, turn them off, please, people. You
might think you already have, but we are all so used to them now
that sometimes we forget, and consequently a cell phone can go off
at just the wrong time, and ruin the whole moment . . . And now
it's my great pleasure to — *(Stops, then impulsively leaves her position
by the table.)* Except I want to say this. I *hate* having to make the
cell-phone speech. It gets everything off on the wrong foot. It makes
me the cop, and you the culprits, and we should all be on the same
footing, especially tonight. Maybe one of these days I'll no longer
have to make that speech. Maybe some day, we'll turn them off

automatically. Or not even bring them. Maybe we'll learn not to bring them to class, either. I hear that Professor Klein in Chemistry docks your grade if your cell phones goes off during his lectures. You should also know that the Athletic Department has a new rule about them. No cell phones if you are participating in an athletic event. Apparently some girl on the cross country team stopped to answer her cell in the middle of a race! And last week a cell phone went off during a Quaker meeting in our interdenominational chapel. Now in Quaker meetings you're supposed to be quiet unless the Holy Spirit moves you. Well, it sure wasn't the Holy Spirit on that cell. It was a Quaker's room-mate looking for the remote to their TV! *(Looks up and off.)* I know, I know. They're waiting. But I'm the head of the lecture committee, and I'm on a roll here. *(To audience.)* Because I don't think cell phones should be allowed at meals. And I'm not just talking about the college cafeteria either. I mean restaurants, too. And in your own home. A meal is a sacred thing. Professor Kibel in Literature says that when we break bread together we remind ourselves of our common nature. He read us that part in *The Iliad* when Priam, the doomed old King of Troy, comes to beg Achilles for the body of his son Hector, whom Achilles has killed and dragged around the city walls. So Priam begs for the body, and Achilles gives it up, and then what happens? They sit down together and share a leg of lamb! The father and the murderer of his son! It's extremely moving. *(She gets teary.)* It says that life must go on, even after a situation like that! So when people start chattering on their cell phones while they eat, they're saying that something more important than the meal is going on somewhere else, which is wrong, because eating together is the heart of the matter. So no phones at meals, please. We should make that a rule. *(A slight pause only.)* And I don't think we should use cell phones when we're walking down the street, either. Why? Because when we're walking places, we should be noticing our surroundings, and greeting people we know, and how can we do that if we're jabbering away on our cells. That means we're out of it, we're elsewhere, and so we bump into people. Or ignore them, which is worse. One time I was walking through the Student Union plaza, and everyone there was either talking on cell phones or listening to their iPods. No one was noticing anyone else. It was like being in a zombie movie like *The Dawn of the Dead.* I wanted to shout out, "Hey, look! I'm here, I'm alive, I'm a human being!" I was so upset when I got to philosophy class that I mentioned this to my teacher, and you know what she said? She said that cell phones are undermining our sense of what the Greeks called the *polis,* which is the basic building block of democracy. She said we need to remind ourselves constantly of our common interconnectedness. That's why we have the agora, or the piazza, or the village square, or Main Street, or right here, in this theater, and if we lose all that, democracy goes right out the window. So we've got to make rules here. We've got to restrict cell phones. As we did with spitting. Or cigarettes. Because we're really talking about civility here. That's what we're really talking about. O K? O K. *(Returns to stand by her table.)* And now it is my great pleasure to introduce a man and a woman who began their journey to worldwide acclaim right here at this very university, and who need no introduction beyond that. May we welcome, please . . . well, they've asked that we call them simply Alice and Dexter!

POST-OEDIPUS
Steven Gridley

Dramatic
Ismene, twenties

> *Here, Ismene talks in direct address to the audience about why her*
> *death may be necessary to save Thebes from a terrible fate.*

ISMENE: OK.

> *(Ismene pulls out a chart with escape and suicide listed at the top.)*

Escaping vs. Staying. If I stayed I would certainly have to die.
My death is required to save the city. So this basically boils down to
Escaping vs. Suicide, which basically boils down to Life vs. Death.
And of course all living beings want to live. So the answer would seem
simple. Here . . . I cross the sea, start a new life, settle down, and
forget all about Thebes. But I will live with the knowledge that I am
responsible for the destruction of the city, since I was not sacrificed
as prophesied. Still I cannot be blamed for my survival instinct. On
this side I won't live longer. I will die. I don't know what happens
after death, could be anything, so that's an unknown. However, I will
die with the knowledge that I saved Thebes. I will probably be re-
garded as a hero. I won't be known as Ismene the quiet nobody. I will
be Ismene the savior of Thebes. *(Pause.)* The irony is not lost on me
that for my life to have any meaning whatsoever . . . I must end it.
Yes. I see that now. Unfortunately, that is the fate of all the weak and
frail in this world. Our only statement in life is our death. How did
they die? I can either die heroically, here, in defense of my city, or I
can die cowardly, far away, old, having perfected the recorder. There-
fore (and I'm nearing the end here) the Life vs. Death struggle basically boils down to *(Shows a new chart with the same words:)* "What
is life for Ismene?" *(Pause.)* My mother . . . never spoke my name,
not once, until just now, in that last scene. She said my name. She
said it three times. I think that I've been dead for years already and
only now, having been given a purpose, can I say that I'm feeling any-

thing inside me that could be called life. So this question basically boiled down to *(Another chart.)* "What has meaning?" *(Pause.)* Yes, I can see now why it is me who should die. I can see why the prophet pointed at me. I am the one . . . without meaning.

PRINCIPIA
Michael Maiello

Comic
Eris, could be any age

*Eris is a goddess, the embodiment of chaos. She has appeared to Bob
and Kerry, two security guards at a dog food factory. Kerry has found
the Golden Apple of the Hesperides, symbol of all the chaos in the
universe. This is the apple that caused the Trojan War. Eris wants
it back.*

ERIS: I am the goddess with the icy dagger in her bosom. And that's rough
on the bosom. Oh, I've suffered. Oh, I've made my mark. Oh, I've
whipped this world around on a string. *(Turns to Kerry.)* You, mortal, have something that belongs to me.

. . . Its power will confound you. Its place in history would leave
you breathless. It is mine, the Golden Apple of the Hesperides,
guarded over by Atlas, stolen by Paris and used by me to spark the
Trojan War.

. . . Kalliste — for the prettiest one. This is how I sparked the
Trojan War. See, they had a party on Olympus and they didn't invite
me. This is the doctrine of the original snub. So I picked up this bauble
and tossed it among the gods. When Hera, Aphrodite, and Athene
saw it, they fought to possess it. They picked a mortal named
Paris — don't ask me why a Trojan prince had a French name, I did-
n't do it — to choose between them. Paris granted it to Aphrodite in
exchange for the love of Helen, who was already hitched. Her face
launched 997 ships, a figure rounded up by the poets. A war happened. My fault. Lots of people died. Achilles took an arrow to an
ankle. These are myths. Lies spun by the media of the time. An at-
tempt to explain to the families back home why the Greeks would
lay siege on a walled city for years and years when they could have
just tried the door. So we have the apple, and we have jealousy, and
we have chaos at the root of it all. I shouldered all the blame and enjoyed the solace of a hot dog with no bun, such was the pain of the
original snub. Do you really believe that?

RELATIVITY
Cassandra Medley

Dramatic
Iris, fifty

> *Iris, a renowned geneticist, is addressing her lab staff (the audience),
> giving us a pep talk but warning that she will continue to be
> extremely demanding.*

IRIS: First off, I've sent out the press release, and I regret to announce the
death of the last kidney transplant animal in your . . . our study.
(Pause.) But don't lose faith — the rodents lived for eight days. It may
not seem like a very long time; but what you've done is quite revo-
lutionary. I'm looking forward to our continuing. *(Pause.)* OK. I'm
not going to offer my "Congratulations" to the seven chosen for my
Special Projects Team. You need no "congratulations." Every single one
of you is used to being "chosen" as top of your class, as *Phi Beta* this,
and that, and for all the top prizes. You're used to being told how
"gifted" you are, it should come as no surprise. *(Pause.)* Now, you all
know I'm known for being tough, you know I don't play favor-
ites . . . any and all rumors that you've heard about me are most likely,
true . . . I will work your butts off and then some, I *do* rollerblade
three miles every morning before work — how many go in for "Starbucks double shot cappuccino"? *(Counts hands.)* People after my own
heart. And it's true, I *do* watch the soaps in my office from two PM
until three PM. Amazingly, so much stupidity helps me think better
afterwards. *(Pause.)* Now, we'll follow the same lab protocol as Doctor Gordon, And I'll take all questions later. *(Pause.)* But, this is what
I want to know, right here, right now. *(Pause.)* Why are you working here? Hum? *(Pause.)* Is it to try to be in on the patents for as many
gene sequences as you can, so as to build up your stock portfolio?
(Glances around.) Is just to go through the motions while you dream
of building your retirement home in Tahiti? Or, do you *really* love
science? See, I plan to work with you all very closely, and I'm going

to watch you. And above all, I have one, non-negotiable demand. That you love science. *(Pause.)* That you love what you do. That you bless the day you found your way to this profession, which will give you your own special place in history! *(Pause.)* That's right, you heard me, and if you think this question's corny, then we're going to have "a problem." *(Pause.)* Do you truly *love* what you do? Do you wake up mornings rain or shine and race to get to the lab? Do you keep polishing our sense of wonder and amazement? Do you cultivate what Einstein referred to as — "holy curiosity"? Do you? *Do* you? *(Lights cross-fade.)*

RESTORING THE SUN
Joe Sutton

Dramatic
Laura, thirties

> *Laura is a science reporter, here talking to Len, a business consultant who specializes in predicting the future, about why his clients were wrong about their claims to have effected cold fusion.*

LAURA: Do you believe that tom-toms restore the sun after an eclipse?

    . . . And better still, how do you argue with someone, an ancient man say, when he tells you that hundreds of experiments have proven that very fact?

    . . . It's a fallacy, Len. But because it's never been tested, it's never been disproved. Ancient man believes the beating of tom-toms will restore the sun and so he beats the tom-toms. And the sun, in every instance, is restored. *(By now she is speaking very quickly, almost without pause.)* But he never tries not beating the tom-toms and instead taking a bath. Or slaughtering his animals. Or playing his flute. If he had, he would have seen the sun was restored in exactly the same number of instances. In other words, the action of slaughtering the animal or playing the flute or beating the tom-tom had NOTHING to do with restoring the sun. The action was unrelated to the outcome. And that fact is determined by running control experiments. By altering the experimental variable to see if it in fact alters the outcome. But your guys didn't do that. They thought that running a current through deuterated water would result in fusion. But they never tried running it through regular water, through *tap* water. If they had, they might have discovered something entirely different.

    . . . That they didn't have fusion, that what they "thought" was fusion, the heat they thought was fusion was actually something else. Because fusion requires neutrons, Len, and hydrogen doesn't have one. Hydrogen, "H", the "H" of H_2O, has no neutrons and so if they're getting heat from tap water . . . it has to be something other than fusion. *(Slight beat.)* And so that's the control you would want to run. You would want to see if you got fusion from regular water.

RESTORING THE SUN
Joe Sutton

Dramatic
Laura, thirties

*Laura is a science reporter, here telling an electrochemist who has
claimed to have effected cold fusion how and why he went wrong.*

LAURA: I think you made a mistake.
(She waits for a response — then . . .)
I think you saw something, or thought you did, and you got
very excited. I think you'd confirmed what you'd long suspected. You
had a theory, a pet theory, and here was the evidence to support it.
And you called out. You called out in excitement. And that's where
you made your mistake. *(A brief pause.)* Because instead of having
someone there who could calm you, who could reason with you, who
could show you where you'd made your mistake, you had Professor
Stevens, a man who had no interest in pulling you back. Quite the
contrary, in fact. *(By now, on a roll.)* He wanted you to go forward.
he wanted you to continue with a process that for him had no
bounds. Because if you were excited, he was beside himself. He was
convinced you were on the road to the Nobel, a prize he had never
before DREAMED for himself. And so he pushed you. He pushed
you continuously. He pushed you to make claims and stake out po-
sitions that you had no way of supporting. And so you counseled
restraint. You . . . But every time you did so, he pushed even harder.
He belittled you. He demanded that you buck up, have courage. Until
one day you found yourself boxed in. *(At this point, she slows.)* By
this time, you'd made claims in writing, in print, that you couldn't
possibly walk away from. And so you had to stick to them. Even if
it meant being uncovered, unmasked . . . *(Really taking her time
now.)* . . . having your entire career called into question. Everything
that has puzzled everyone that has ever known you . . . or written
about you . . . over the last forty years. . .*(She then pauses, allowing
what she has said to settle in. Then . . .)* That's why I think you did
it. why you continue to do it . . . I don't know.

SHOUT!
Phillip George and Peter Charles Morris

Comic
Red Girl, twenties

> Shout! *is a "bird's-eye view" of the Swinging 60s in England. In-*
> *terpersed between hit songs of the period are monologues for each of*
> *the characters, who are defined by the color of their costumes. Here*
> *the "Red Girl," something of a geek, is writing in to a fan maga-*
> *zine about how she got all tarted up to nab a bloke named Edward.*

RED GIRL: "My Most Embarrassing Moment" by Miss X. It all started when I went to an Italian film with Edward. I was certain he had dishonorable intentions. I sat through *La Dolce Vita* with my arms folded across my chest so he couldn't fondle my charlies.

. . . Well, he didn't touch them. Never even tried. Spent the whole night goggling Anita Ekberg.

. . . I decided if that's the kind of woman men like, that's the kind of woman I'll be. I bought myself a blond Dynel wig and stuffed my brassiere with tissues. I put on blue eye shadow and white lipstick. I swung my hips as I slunk my way down the King's Road.

. . . "Won't Edward be surprised?" I thought to myself.

. . . Only I was the one who got surprised. I was arrested for solicitation.

. . . When Edward saw me in the jail cell, he laughed so hard he practically peed himself. I was so embarrassed. I started crying. I had to take a tissue from my brassiere to wipe the tears. That's when Edward reached through the bars, touched my shoulder and said, "Don't be a fool, love, I liked you the way you were." That's when I let him fondle my charlies.

SHOUT!
Phillip George and Peter Charles Morris

Comic
Green Girl, twenties

> Shout! *is a "bird's-eye view" of the Swinging 60s in England. Interpersed between hit songs of the period are monologues for each of the characters, who are defined by the color of their costumes. Here the "Green Girl" talks about the many ingeniously devious ways to dump a bloke.*

GREEN GIRL: *(Reading magazine.)* According to this survey, "73% of women experience some form of anxiety when severing relations with men."

(She laughs and tosses magazine aside.)

I don't care what the studies say, breaking up is NOT hard to do. I do it all the time. The trick is knowing what method to use on what bloke. If 'e's the Cambridge and Oxford type, be rational.

(Sweetly.)

"It's not you, love. It's me. You're port wine and paté, and I'm meat pies and ale. It would never work." No. Don't speak. Just go.

(She speaks normally again.)

See what I mean? But if 'e's one of those East End blokes, an all-out attack works best.

(Hysterical.)

"You're shagging that tart, aren't you!

(She mimes throwing something.)

Don't you lie to me! I saw you give 'er the eye!

. . . I can't take this anymore! It's tearing me apart!"

. . . And he's out the door before the poor blighter knows what 'it 'im.

. . . Now, breaking up with one of those sweet, sensitive chaps is a bit trickier. It's best to just come right out with it and lie.

(Melodramatic.)

"The doctor says six months at most."

(She coughs.)

"It'll be a painful, messy death. I couldn't put you through it. Pray for me."

(She coughs him out the door.)

Oh, and if 'e's American, just get fat. 'E'll break up with you.

SOMEBODY'S SOMEBODY
Gary Richards

Dramatic
Linda, forty

Linda is speaking to her husband, who has hit her for the very last time.

LINDA: You used to make me feel safe. You used to put your arms around me and there was no other place in the world I'd rather be.

. . . You used to tell me that you were going to take care of me.

. . . And over the years I convinced myself that you made me feel safe. No matter what happened. And for a while, you did. When the kids were babies, and I was young, and you were doing well, I think I was happy and safe. I never regretted dropping out of college and being your wife. I always felt it was in the stars. It was exactly what I was supposed to do, what I was put on this Earth for. My calling. The homecoming queen marries the captain of the football team and has babies. I was living a dream, a lucky, lucky girl. My children needed me, my husband loved me . . .

. . . things were pretty much going the way I had expected them to go. Picnics on the Fourth of July. Cranberry sauce on Thanksgiving. Midnight Mass on Christmas Eve. I remember many moments thinking "it doesn't get any better than this." *(Linda turns to Tom.)* I'm so happy I was aware of those moments as they were happening. And grateful for them. Because it didn't get any better. It got worse. It was all a setup . . .

. . . a setup for right now. I was set up to fail. My life was set up to be disappointing! I *was* the homecoming queen. I *was* the salutatorian. I *was* Tommy Gulotta's girlfriend. What am I now?! What am I now?! Look at me! Look at me! My world was ideal back then! I lived in a perfect world! "Most Likely to Succeed." At what?! Being a punching bag?! *(Pause.)*

. . . My bruises will heal. My pain will not last forever. I WILL NOT LET IT!! I refuse to fear the future, the next time you raise your hand and hit me again.

THEY'RE JUST LIKE US
Boo Killebrew

Dramatic
Beth, late twenties to mid-thirties

> *Beth, an actress, is doing a press conference for her latest film. She is very adept at playing the role of "Movie Star," not so adept at hiding her real self.*

BETH: Tim saw me doing that play and decided to call me in. I was told that this movie was a vehicle for Biz and that they needed a really strong character actress to play his mother in the flashback scenes. The audition went really well, I told them I didn't mind gaining the weight for the part, and the rest is history. *(Listens to the reporters.)* I gained one hundred and seven pounds. *(Listens.)* Lots of donuts! *(Laughs. Listens.)* Well, thank you very much. Yeah, it just came right off, I have a very high metabolism. *(Listens.)* Yes, it was very tough from time to time. It was a pretty intense role, and I tend to really dive into characters and sometimes it can be really difficult to go there. I wouldn't have it any other way, though. You know, in order for me to really explore a character, I have to explore some areas of myself that have been neglected or are unknown and that can be scary. *(Listens.)* Oh, you had to squeeze that one in didn't you? I know everyone is talking about us, so it's OK. Yes, we are officially over. *(Listens.)* I did take my experience in my relationships into account when exploring this role. That was very hard, yes. *(Listens.)* I do not keep in touch with him, no. He doesn't talk to me anymore. I tried, but after a while, you have to hold onto your dignity. I don't ever want to beg anyone, and it got to that point. I was begging. And then you think, begging for what? *(Loses focus.)* Begging to be silently judged by this person every minute of every day? Begging to feel guilty about caring about yourself and your career? Begging to feel like you are secretly hated by him? To feel a lump in your throat every time you sit down to eat? To wake up at five AM, sweaty and sticky and panicked that this could be the day that he leaves you? To know that that person will leave you one day? To know that this person will leave you? They will leave you and they will not remember you. *(Snaps out of it.)* I'm sorry, I just get passionate — sorry. So, I stopped trying. This is life, you have to move on and be thankful for what you have. My career is just getting started and I have a very full life. I do wish him well, though. I will always wish him nothing but happiness. *(Listens.)* Thank you. That's very nice of you. Thank you very much.

THEY'RE JUST LIKE US
Boo Killebrew

Seriocomic
Beth, late twenties to mid-thirties

Beth is a movie actress, here pretending to be giving an interview to Barbara Walters. She could be practicing for an actual scheduled interview, or this could just be a moment of fantasy.

BETH: Well, you know it's difficult, absolutely. He is now in the land of roads and space and I suppose his world is good for him and my world is good for me. It's very hard to be in this business and have a relationship. I mean, you know this — we all know this. Some people make it. A lot of people do not. *(Pauses to listen.)* You know, Barbara, sometimes I do wonder if it is worth it. I do miss him. I guess I am a woman who needs to float. I do miss him, though. I miss getting a beer with him in the early evening. *(Begins to lose focus and sort of begins a rant.)* I miss his tired eyes. I miss his pretty hands, he had such pretty hands. I miss feeling like I could actually have a beautiful, deep relationship. *(Snaps out of it.)* Whoa . . . looks like the romantic in me got carried away there for a second! No, I was sick of apologizing for my choice and for my success every single day. *(Listens.)* Barbara, there are days when I think you are right. Days when I think that I will find someone who will be comfortable with my life . . . other days I think maybe it's just fine that I am going to be by myself. I've got it pretty good. Men may come and go, but I will always be standing right by my side. And I think that me is not such a bad thing. *(Listens.)* Yes, it was his decision, but I guess I sort of silently made it as well. *(Listens.)* I do wonder if I could have gone back and taken a different route, would I be happier? *(Loses focus again.)* Would I be able to think of the day I die without panicking that I might be the only one with me? Would I be able to slow down? And then I think, "No. I wouldn't change a thing. Honestly, I really love my life and I wouldn't change a thing." *(She is quiet.)* I do miss him, though. *(She is quiet. She stops the interview.)* This is stupid. I am so stupid.

THEY'RE JUST LIKE US
Boo Killebrew

Dramatic
Liz, elderly

> *Liz has become increasingly obsessed with being forgotten after she
> is gone. Here, she is focusing on a particular person, an old lover
> perhaps.*

LIZ: How can I make you remember me? A tin box! I could hide an old
tin box in the hole of a tree and I could put pictures and little toys
and letters and poems in the box and a young explorer would find it
and wonder who I was. Someone would say that you knew me. That
if they wanted to know about me, they could ask you. You would be
old. You would be old and they would ring your doorbell and you
would open the door. You invite the explorer in. You sit him down.
He hands you the box. You put on your old-man glasses. You are old.
You open the box and you are excited again. You open the box and
see a picture of me. I am smiling with my lips shut. My eyes are bright.
I am laughing at something in my head. You are back with me. I was
a great mystery. You remember how you couldn't keep me and you
smile. The explorer sees that you remember and he begins to ask you
questions about me. You answer. You say you can't remember why it
didn't work out, but that I was a beautiful creature who needed to
float. That's all you can remember. And you loved that about me. It
broke your heart, but you loved that about me.

TROUT STANLEY
Claudia Dey

Dramatic
Grace, late twenties to early thirties

Grace is fiercely protective of her agoraphobic twin sister Sugar, who lives with her in a trailer. Here she is talking about Sugar to a mysterious drifter named Trout Stanley, who might be a threat.

GRACE: Garbage is tea leaves, is tarot cards, is crystal balls. That's what the Holy Father said. An' he was right. I knew everything that happens in this town Trout Stanley. Garbage tells me everything. Garbage is the mos' truthful story I ever heard.

. . . The stink. It's humanity. An' people who're scared o' the stink are scared o' humanity. I for one am not. Sugar thinks I'm vain. That all I care about is this. My mane, my dynamite outfits, my classic-cut rodeo-style cowboys boots. Bullroar. Sure, sometimes bein' in the Boutique Christmas catalogues goes to my head. Boutique head, you know. Billboard head. Floatin' a little through town. 'Specially when I catch a glimpse o' myself in the backroom at the SuperSavers or pinned up in the fire station, guys crowded around my calendar. I like it. I like the attention. I like bein' liked. I like bein' looked at. But I don' need it. I got other things. Other dreams. Other secrets. I got a million, Trout. Sugar an' her tragedies. She thinks I don' know the grisly side o' life. Well I do. Whatever's happened to her has happened to me too.

. . . I love one thing. An' it's Sugar. Sugar's my life . . . Ten years ago, the Holy Mother was struck by a fever. She had a temperature of 106 degrees. That's hotter'n India Trout, hotter'n Greece, . . . hotter'n the fire in your pants —

. . . Sugar's out. The Holy Mother lay in her bed. Burnin' like a coil. Holy Father wouldn' let the doctors in. Sayin' they're all quacks. So we watched her day an' night. On rotation. Gave her ice baths, ice water, love. She jus' thrashed in her sheets sayin' weird, sometimes terrible, sometimes beautiful things, feverish things. She even spoke to our dear dead Ducklin' — though she didn' call her that. She called her Angel. *Angel.* Sugar never heard it; neither did the Holy Father. Jus' me. Angel.

Durin' the day, the Holy Father an' I would go to the Dump. Try to keep livin'. Normal life. Well I hate Normal an' I'm pretty sure Normal hates me. We come home the afternoon of our twentieth birthday an' there's Sugar sittin' on the Holy Mother's bed, glowin' like a jack-o'-lantern.

. . . The Holy Mother had died jus' moments before. Sugar's the las' to touch her; the heat spreads through her like the Tropics an' it fills her with a low-burnin' orange. She looks like a leaf held upside the sun. Can see all her veins. Her eyes are fireballs.

The Holy Father is come over with a terrible grief. He starts to yowl an' shake. Suddenly he takes off into the Pines. Are we gonna lose him too? Whole town forms a search party, out in their bug suits, flashlights sweepin' like meteor showers, cops twistin' their moustaches into pipe cleaners, whole teams o' dogs, whole teams o' everyone, shoutin', sniffin', scourin', eyes fixed to the groun' . . . an' then Sugar comes between us with a superior quiet — partin' the Red Sea an' leadin' us, our Laura Secord, leadin' us to him, to the Holy Father. An' there he was, split by lightnin'. Like an axe to wood. Split perfect in two. Standin' under the tallest tree. Tree an echo o' what he is. Split. Perfect. Funny thing is, it was the cleares' night o' the year. Not a cloud in the sky . . . An' there we were, made orphans in a night.

This is why we make promises Trout. 'Cause promises gave us somethin' to believe in, somethin' to hold onto. Somethin' sure. Otherwise we're all jus' circlin' the earth wonderin' where it's safe to land . . .

Night before the Holy Mother dies she makes me swear on everything that I will protect Sugar with my life. "Promise that you will take care of your sister Grace, for she is prized. Between you, me, an' the above an' beyond, if we had to pin a ribbon on one o' ya, it'd be Sugar. Sugar has a future." An' what do I have, I asked the Holy Mother, her eyes flutterin' like tired butterflies. "You have Sugar," she said, "you have Sugar." That's the last conversation we had. Some might say my mother was cruel. I say she was jus' sayin' it like it is.

An' that's what I'm doin' Trout Stanley: I'm protectin' Sugar. I'm protectin' Sugar with my life. She's an easy target. She's the perfect prey. An' people who take advantage, they're stacked in the woods.

UNCLE JACK
Jeff Cohen

Dramatic
Sophie, twenties

> Uncle Jack *is an updated adaptation of* Uncle Vanya. *Sophie is defending Dr. Ashe's dedication to protecting the environment. She is speaking to Helena, Dr. Ashe, her Uncle Jack, and others. Her new stepmother Helena is a former runway model visiting West Virginia from New York City who cannot understand Ashe's devotion to preserving the forests of West Virginia.*

SOPHIE: No, Helena, it's hardly silly. And hardly boring. That's just ignorant. Tending to the resources of the forests is about the most important work there is. When Michael plants and cares for new trees he's giving something back to a planet that is being destroyed at an alarming rate. Perhaps that doesn't occur to you in the city. Michael's work has been recognized, he's too modest to say so but he's been given citations by the Department of the Interior and the Audubon Society for his work. It's people like Michael who are the heroes, who save the environment when people in the city are too busy reading *Vogue* and taking taxis to Starbucks. We here in the country recognize that his work is a very noble calling. These trees, these national forests, they are the lungs of our planet. But even more than that they are a graceful and glorious reminder of how beautiful and sacred is the abundance of the natural world and how ugly and wasteful and destructive we are in it. I see Michael's work as embodying a type of latter-day chivalry. I'm afraid this is a foreign concept to you because in the city you have nothing like it and your lives are aggressive and nasty and cutthroat. But not here. Here in the midst of arbors, in the shadows of the great trees, our lives are gentler, kinder, with a greater sense of spirituality, a greater sense of calm. Men like Michael, who devote themselves to forestry, I think are more masculine, they are handsome, there is a natural grace that flows through them. You don't hear about women being beaten and raped and mistreated here the way they are in cities. Michael embodies this chivalry. He is a Knight of the Arbors!

VICTORIA MARTIN: MATH TEAM QUEEN

Kathryn Walat

Seriocomic
Victoria, teens

> *Victoria is a high school student who's interested mostly in being popular. She thinks the math team is a bunch of geeks, and she is not altogether sure she wants to join them.*

VICTORIA: I'm *popular*. Like totally, undisputedly popular. Like, I walk down the hallways, and even though I'm a sophomore, there are seniors — senior *guys*, with deep voices — who say: *Hey.* Sometimes they say: *Hey, Vickie, what's up?* Like, they know my name.

OK, so mostly they're on the basketball team so they know my boyfriend, who is totally varsity first string, even though he's only a junior, because this fall while the other guys were playing football all he did was practice his free-throws, because he's a one-sport guy. Scott. He's totally into me. And that's why I'm a *sophomore* and those senior jocks know my *name,* but it's not like I'm one of those slutty girls whose names all the guys know, and plus I totally have girlfriends too.

I'm friends with the *Jens.* Who are on the varsity cheerleading squad, even though they're sophomores, mostly because all the juniors who tried out this year had "weight issues" so forget trying to get *them* up in a pyramid — plus, the Jens are very, very peppy. They know how to do that thing where they toss their ponytails, and depending on the toss, it's either like: What*ever*, I am so walking away from *you*. Or, it's like: See this swish? That's right, this ponytail says: I will see *you* later.

I understand this distinction. I am not a cheerleader. But I *know* this. I have secured my place in the high school universe, after the very volatile freshman year, which the Jens and I refer to as: Versaille. Like, the Treaty of Versaille? You know — World War I, European power struggle, third period history with Mr. Delano — that's where we met, our desks, in a row, across the back of the room: Jen-Me-Jen.

Yesterday at the math meet? All of that was suddenly meaningless. This one kid had an equation on his T-shirt. The quadratic formula, across his back. I *know!* I mean, nerd central, *all* math geeks, *and* I was the only girl. Except for these two on the other team, who would only speak to each other. In binary. For fun. And when I was in the girls' bathroom and I totally just got my period, and had to ask one of them for a pad, they just *giggled.* And so I had to stuff all of this scratchy school-grade toilet paper into my underwear and meanwhile, I almost missed the sophomore round of questions, because they put all the room numbers in Roman numerals. For fun. And when I finally got there, I was sitting up next to this kid, who kept clicking his retainer, and it was driving me crazy, and I was like —

(Suddenly the rest of the team is there. She turns and speaks to them.)

I don't *do* headgear, OK?

VICTORIA MARTIN: MATH TEAM QUEEN

Kathryn Walat

Dramatic
Victoria, teens

> *Victoria has recently joined her high school's math team and has be-*
> *come friends with the team's captain, Peter, to whom this is addressed.*

VICTORIA: My dad was supposed to teach me how to drive. But he's in California right now. He got this awesome computer-programming job. He used to work from home, designing software, but my mother says he wasn't any good because he never thought about the *people* who would be *using* the software. He's the smartest man my mom ever met. But at the end of the day, which is like my mom's favorite expression: "At the end of the day . . ." his *brain* wasn't enough.

He moved away on this really hot day at the end of last summer, and all of a sudden I was like a sophomore at this big opening game party, which I only went to because the Jens said we should totally go and my mom said I should get out of the house, and I felt kinda stupid and I drank this nasty punch and then I felt really weird and I was sitting outside on the curb, and Scott Sumner said he would give me a ride home — I think he was feeling left out or something because he doesn't play a fall sport — and we made out in his car and then he called me the next day because I left my jacket in his car, and then by Monday Jen — or Jen — I forget which one, said that we were dating.

So we would hang out together after school, me and Scott, those last warm afternoons in October, while the other guys were at football or soccer practice and the Jens were doing cheerleading squad. We would drive down by Weber Pond — it's so pretty there — and make out in his car, or just sit there and watch the yellow leaves floating on the water and everything would just — slow down.

We didn't really talk about my dad. I mean, he knew my

parents were separated and stuff. He hates his dad. They get in fights like after every basketball game. Basketball is really important to Scott. He would always talk about how he just wanted his game to get better and better.

I just wanted to survive. To make it through the school year to the summer, when I could go to California, where no one would know who I was. Except my dad. Who knows what I like without even asking, like pizza with sausage and broccoli, and reruns of *The Honeymooners,* and numbers. I guess what I really like are numbers. But then I would think *numbers* are stupid to like. Because, in high school, what can you do with numbers?

. . . But now, it's sorta different.

. . . Like, at the meet on Wednesday? I was in the middle of that totally nasty multi-variable algebraic equation, and I was almost freaking out —

. . . So I'm like wiping my palms on my jeans just so I can hold my pencil. And all I can hear is the breathing of that red-haired kid with asthma. In and out. In and out — and it's like I can't *stop* listening because I swear any second he's gonna *stop breathing,* and I totally cut gym class the day we had that CPR stuff.

But then I just start moving my pencil. Fast. I pretend like it's the brush of that guy on that painting show — do you ever watch that after school? Scratch, scratch, scratch, and I don't know where I'm headed, I'm just *doing* it — substituting in, distributing — stabbing at it through the mist, like when that artist guy makes a stroke of color across the white canvas, and you think: How the heck is he gonna make a mountain scene out of *that?*

. . . And suddenly, the equation starts to look like something else, right?

. . . Something new, in terms of *y,* and then I know *exactly* where I'm going.

. . . It's like, I can see the steps in front of me, and I just keep stepping and stepping and . . .

. . . And I have no idea if the kid with asthma is breathing or what, and I don't care.

. . . And you know what? That whole time I didn't once think about my dad in California, or the Jens at cheerleading practice, or failing English class. In my head it's like yellow leaves floating on Weber Pond. Like the numbers have — stopped. I think that's what it must feel like, when Pi ends.

THE WATER'S EDGE
Theresa Rebeck

Dramatic
Helen, forties

*Many years ago one of Helen's children, a toddler, drowned. Helen
has always blamed her husband, who left her and whom she has not
seen or heard from in many years, for the death of her child. He has
inexplicably returned, and Helen is telling her two surviving children, both adults now, why she can never forgive what happened.*

HELEN: No. NO. You are not allowed to say that. An accident is you look
away for one moment, half a moment, that's a — He didn't even
know it had happened! How long was she in there? How —
    (Beat. To Lucy.)
    I was the one who found her. He didn't even know. If you go
down, in the morning. You'll see. The light on the water, it moves
on the trees, everything moves, all those subtle greens, it's quite
strange, really, everything seems to be moving but nothing, it's a trick
of the light on the water. On this side, not — the reflection of the
trees across the lake, they're black, almost, the sun is behind them
so the shadow cast across the lake is, and then, the lily pads, on the
shadow, they pick up the sun, each one so flat and white, and — it
was — you don't, you have no — I'm sorry, what —
    . . . No! I'm explaining something! The light. After all this time
it's still the same after all this time, you can go down and look. I can
stand to look. Because she's not there, is she. To see that, in the water.
So sure that it must be impossible. She's with Richard. That's not
your child. It's a trick of the light.

THE WATER'S EDGE
Theresa Rebeck

Dramatic
Helen, forties

*Many years ago one of Helen's children, a toddler, drowned. Helen
has always blamed her husband, who left her and whom she has not
seen or heard from in many years, for the death of her child. He has
inexplicably returned, and Helen is telling her two surviving children, both adults now, and her husband's lady friend Lucy why she
can never forgive what happened, and why she killed him.*

HELEN: It didn't have to happen, Erica. I mean, it's not like I went looking for him. And believe me, he knew it would be a mistake to come
back. But he couldn't let it go. You don't understand, you're too
young, and frankly, I've tried to protect you from all of this. So many
things you didn't know. My silence, everything you blame me for,
that was protection, so no, you can't understand. He said, last night,
that he wanted to step back into the center of his nature. That meant,
all of it. All of us. Forgiving him, moving on. He wanted everything,
so many men do. They want their crime and their forgiveness too,
more than forgiveness, they want the earth itself to rise up and erase
the worst of everything they do, no responsibility, action without con-
sequence, everything is still theirs, that's what they want! And I'm
not going to lie to you. Most of them get it. And it's a sin. The era-
sure of justice? We can't survive it. As a people. It has deformed us,
this insistence that men, with their power and their selfishness and
their cruelty can crawl the earth and destroy everything, everything,
and no one holds them to account. Justice? Do you know what kind
of justice I was offered when he murdered my child? The police came,
then, and ruled it an accident. To be told endlessly it was no one's
fault. Last night I heard it all again, he wasn't responsible, he simply went into his head and that's why it happened. Because he was
absorbed in the intricacies of his endlessly fascinating mind, his child

disappeared in the wood, and then into the water, she disappeared from this earth and he was not responsible. How could he help going into his head and worrying about nothing? It wasn't even nothing, to him, even now, it was still important to him, these things in his head, he was telling me, there was someone, at his work, looking to blame him for some loss of revenue, do these words mean anything? To anyone?

(Laughing.)

To him, they still did. He had justification. It wasn't his fault. He offered this to me — seriously — as something that might heal me! He was all concerned, at one time, in my rage I accused him of betraying me, I was hungry, for some absurd meaning, if he had fallen in love, perhaps, his passion led him and all of us astray, that was something, I thought, for a moment, years ago, that might have been a reality, something to explain the inexplicable, how can you let your child drown, before your eyes? How can you do it? And he took that lame hope from me, as a gift, no, there was was no other woman! If there was any blame, it was mine. We should have gone through it together. I was somehow not womanly enough, the failure was mine, I should have risen from the tragedy like an angel and wiped his crime away from his brow. Like a mother. Well, I am a mother. Over time, all this time, that is what I have been, and there has been too much time given to me. You don't know how hard I prayed, year in and year out, for the rage and the bitterness to leave me, for it to grow into some larger meaning, I begged whatever is out there to reveal to me how to move on, I lived with nature, I cared for the children who were left to me as if they were life itself, I held them to me as protection against all of it and still there was nothing! You pray for justice and the gods laugh. You pray for peace and they abandon you. A moment's peace. He had it. That is what he brought here, to me. The sight of his peace. The yearning to be together. Again. To move forward. To leave it behind. Well, I gave him what he wanted. We finished it, together, the only way it could be finished. And I have no remorse. *(Then, to Lucy.)* Call the police. I don't care. I have my peace now, and god knows I've earned it. I'm going to take a bath.

WISHING WELL
Jon Klein

Dramatic
Callie, thirty-nine

*Callie works for an insurance company as a Catastrophe Specialist.
Here, she is speculating (in direct address to the audience) about a
recent Act of God and its implications.*

CALLIE: As you can see — or as, obviously, you can't see — the power is
out. A storm is coming. Some people call this an act of God. The
faithful, of course. And the insurance companies. Who put their faith
in actuarial tables. But they believe in God too. God gives them something to sell. Namely, insurance against the mercurial whims of the
Almighty. Because if God decides to send a lightning bolt into your
bedroom, or feels like diverting a local tributary into your basement,
there's nothing you can do to stop it. Except maybe prayer, if you
think that might work. But either way, you can get your money back.
(She moves closer to the audience.) That's where I come in. I'm a claim
adjuster. Or, to be more precise, a Catastrophe Specialist. My firm
downplays the religious implications. But they exist between the lines.
See, if God has it in for us, then the sensible thing to do is to protect yourself against those few occasions when he decides to "act."
That's when whole reasoning for catastrophic insurance coverage. In-
stitutionalized existentialism. You won't find many Christian Scien-
tists in the insurance industry. *(She sits on the lip of the stage.)* Don't
get me wrong. I love my job. Determining the probability of events.
That's a pretty cool way to play God. If you're so inclined. And I
usually am. Sure, it's a game — but name a better one. Risk? Life?
Mousetrap? No, for the sheer entertainment value, nothing beats playing God. Although there is a bit of a downside. Which would
be . . . oh, I suppose all the exposure to extreme human suffering.
But I do have a generous 401(k) plan. I wonder if God does.
(The thunder rumbles again, louder.)

Anyway, this act of God has just left us in the dark. Literally. So here I wait, outside my mother's house, near the ocean. And God is hovering around up there, deciding whether to simply take our power — or blow us to kingdom come.

(More thunder, getting closer.)

Unless, of course, God is dead. Or too distracted by events in the Middle East to care about what happens on a tiny island off the coast of North Carolina. In which case, this is no act of God. I did it myself. Two days ago. With the wishing well.

WISHING WELL
Jon Klein

Dramatic
Callie, thirty-nine

Callie works for an insurance company as a Catastrophe Specialist. Here, she is talking (in direct address to the audience) about an ex-beau and about what she's recently found of her late father's in the refrigerator.

CALLIE: I know. Believe me, I know. I always knew what I was in for with Dennis. Look how we met. I was doing a claim on his Honda Civic. Which had been crushed by a fallen tree — after being hit by lightning. Naturally, Dennis had predicted "partly cloudy." It seemed like a good fit. I predict the value of disaster — keeping it to a minimum. And he predicts the extent and frequency — also keeping it to a minimum. It may not be the passionate romance I imagined as a lovesick teenager. Or even Cindy's age. But that's OK. There are ways to take refuge in . . . the minimum. *(She leafs through the faded comic books.)* Want to see what I found on the boat? Comic books. Just where I remembered leaving them, in the freezer compartment in my Dad's mini-fridge. Just in case the boat sank. Talk about a self-fulfilling prophecy. Of course, not even a mini-fridge was airtight, so the salt water got to them. by now they're so faded I can barely read the titles. *Nancy. Little Lulu. Heidi. Little Orphan Annie.* Hmm. I sense a pattern here. *(She pulls a sheet of paper out from inside one of them. She squints at it.)* What's this? A drawing? A letter? Can't tell. Is that the word "you"? Was I writing "I love you" to my Dad? Maybe he was writing to me. Maybe . . . maybe nothing. *(She puts it back, and puts the stack down on a table.)* Whatever it means, it's been in a broken freezer for nineteen years. Which didn't keep it safe, or dry, or legible. It meant something then. But not any more. I guess there's no such thing as a "frozen" moment.

WOMAN BEFORE A GLASS
Lanie Robertson

Dramatic
Peggy, sixties

> *This is a one-woman play about the visionary art collector Peggy
> Guggenheim that takes place in her mansion in Venice. Here, she is
> talking about a meeting with a famed art critic, and about how she
> learned from him about what constitutes great art.*

PEGGY: There was a very old critic here
named Berenson . . .
who spent most of his life
studying the paintings in Venice.
The Bellinis,
Tintoretto,
Veronese, Titian,
and my favorite artist Giorgione.
I met the old man
and invited him here.
He said, "Oh no, Mrs. Guggenheim,
your pictures would upset my stomach."

I told him if he'd only come I'd turn everyone one of them to the wall.
He was a hero to me.
I'd read all he'd ever written 'cause Laurence Vail
said I wasn't intelligent enough
to understand Bernard Berenson, so I read them all.
Seven volumes.

And I learned from him what makes a painting great.
The line.
The quality of color.
The tactile value, et cetera.

The unity of tone, et cetera.

The painter's soul, his anima reflected in the paint, et cetera.

How the work of a particular painter relates to that of the other artists of his time, et cetera, et cetera.

So I was so excited when he agreed to come
I had all the pictures covered or turned to the wall,
and sent one of my gondoliers to bring him here.

And I went to the front of the house to watch for him on the Grand Canal.

And when I saw my gondola approaching
I was standing beside the huge equestrian statue
Marino Marini made for me called, "The Angel of the City."
It's a young, virile man on horseback
and greeting the world and life — with his arms flung out like this.
And his phallus, huge and erect,
filled with
joie d'vivre.

And when I saw Mr. Berenson approaching the house
I shouted, "Mr. Berenson! Here! Up here!"
and I waved and waved.

And suddenly
Guido, my gondolier, stopped rowing.
And then the gondola slowly turned 'round
and went away.

I couldn't believe it.

And Guido said
Berenson had ordered him to take him back.

He said, "Tell Mrs. Guggenheim,
unless she covers that huge phallus,
and hides it from public view,
I'll never come there again."

Perhaps that's the answer.

The real answer.

Perhaps it's just . . .
uncovering the phallus after all.

RIGHTS AND PERMISSIONS

ALL THIS INTIMACY. © 2006 by Rajiv Joseph. Reprinted by permission of Seth Glewen, The Gersh Agency, 41 Madison Ave., New York, NY 10010. The entire text has been published by Samuel French, Inc., 45 W. 25th St., New York, NY 10010. (www.samuelfrench.com) who also handle performance rights.

ANDROMEDA'S GALAXY. © 2006 by Alan Haehnel. All rights reserved. Reprinted by permission of Playscripts, Inc. To purchase acting editions of this play, or to obtain stock or amateur performance rights, you must contact Playscripts, Inc.: 325 W. 38th St. #315, New York, NY 10018. 866-NEW-PLAY (866-639-7529). Website: www.playscripts.com E-mail: info@playscripts.com

BABY'S BLUES. © 2006 by Tammy Ryan. Reprinted by permission of the author. The entire text has been published by Broadway Play Publishing, Inc., 56 E. 81 st St., New York, NY 10028-8358. 212-772-8334 (www.broadwayplaypubl.com) who also handle performance rights.

BFF. ©2007 by Anna Ziegler. Reprinted by permission of Peregrine Whittlesey, 279 Central Park W. #23, New York, NY 10024. 212-787-1802 (pwwagy@aol.com). The entire text has been published by Smith and Kraus, Inc. in *New Playwrights: The Best Plays of 2007* (www.smithandkraus.com). For performance rights contact Dramatists Play Service, 440 Park Avenue, South, New York, NY 10016, www.dramatists.com, 212-MU3-8960.

BLASTER. © 2006 by Victoria Stewart. All rights reserved. Reprinted by permission of Playscripts, Inc. To purchase acting editions of this play, or to obtain stock or amateur performance rights, you must contact Playscripts, Inc.: 325 W. 38th St. #315, New York, NY 10018. 866-NEW- PLAY (866-639-7529). Website: www.playscripts.com E-mail: info@playscripts.com

BLOOD ORANGE. © 2006 by David Wiener. Reprinted by permission of Ronald Gwiazda, Abrams Artists Agency, 275 7th Ave., New York, NY 10001. The entire text has been published by Dramatists Play Service, 440 Park Ave. S., New York, NY 10016. 212-MU3-8960 (www.dramatists.com). who also handle performance rights.

THE BLOWIN OF BAILE GALL. © 2006 by Ronan Noone. Reprinted by permission of Ronald Gwiazda, Abrams Artists Agency, 275 7th Ave., New York, NY 10001. The entire text has been published by Dramatists Play Service, 440 Park Ave. S., New York, NY 10016. 212-MU3-8960 (www.dramatists.com) who also handle performance rights.

CAROL MULRONEY. © 2006 by Stephen Belber. Reprinted by permission of John Buzzetti, The Gersh Agency, 41 Madison Ave., New York, NY 10010. The entire text has been published by Dramatists Play Service, 440 Park Ave. S., New York, NY 10016. 212-MU3-8960 (www.dramatists.com) who also handle performance rights.

CONVERGENCE. ©2006 by Bryn Manion. Reprinted by permission of the author. The entire text has been published by New York Theatre Experience in *Plays and Playwrights 2007*. (www.nyte.org) For performance rights contact the author c/o NY Theatre Experience via e-mail: info@nyte.org

THE DEAD GUY. © 2005 by Eric Coble. Reprinted by permission of Val Day, William Morris Agency, 1325 Ave. of the Americas, New York, NY 10019. The entire text has been published by Dramatists Play Service, 440 Park Ave. S., New York, NY 10016. 212-MU3-8960 (www.dramatists.com) who also handle performance rights.

DEDICATION; or, THE STUFF OF DREAMS. © 2006 by Terrence McNally. Reprinted by permission of Grove/Atlantic, 841 Broadway, New York, 10003. The entire text has been published by Grove/Atlantic, and in an acting editions by Dramatists Play Service, 440 Park Ave. S., New York, NY 10016. 212-MU3-8960. (www.dramatists.com) who also handle performance rights.

EL PASO BLUES. © 1996 by Octavio Solis. Reprinted by permission of the author. The entire text has been published by Broadway Play Publishing, Inc., 56 E. 81st St., New York, NY 10028-8358. 212-772-8334 (www.broadwayplaypubl.com) who also handle performance rights.

FIRST BAPTIST OF IVY GAP. © 2004, 2006 by Ron Osborne. Reprinted by permission of Samuel French, Inc., 45 W. 25th St., New York, NY 10010. 212-206-8990. (www.samuelfrench.com) who also handle performance rights. The entire text has been published by Samuel French, Inc.

GOING TO THE CHAPEL. © 2004, 2006 by Donald Steele. Reprinted by permission of Samuel French, Inc., 45 W. 25th St., New York, NY 10010. 212-206-8990. (www.samuelfrench.com) who also handle performance rights. The entire text has been published by Samuel French, Inc.

HOME FRONT. © 2006 by Greg Owens. Reprinted by permission of the author. The entire text has been published by Broadway Play Publishing, Inc., 56 E. 81st St., New York, NY 10028-8358. 212-772-8334 (www.broadwayplaypubl.com) who also handle performance rights.

HOW HIS BRIDE CAME TO ABRAHAM. © 2006 by Karen Sunde. Reprinted by permission of the author. The entire text has been published by Broadway Play Publishing, Inc., 56 E. 81st St., New York, NY 10028-8358. 212-772-8334 (www.broadwayplaypubl.com) who also handle performance rights.

INTELLECTUALS. © 2006 by Scott C. Sickles. Reprinted by permission of Barbara Hogenson, 165 West End Ave. #19C, New York, NY 10023. 212-874-8092. (bhogenson@aol1.com). The entire text has been published by Smith and Kraus in *New Playwrights: The Best Plays of 2007* (www.smithandkraus.com). Contact Barbara Hogenson for performance rights.

THE INTELLIGENT DESIGN OF JENNY CHOW. © 2006 by Rolin Jones. Reprinted by permission of Chris Till, Paradigm, 500 5th Ave., New York, NY 10110. The entire text has been published by Dramatists Play Service, 440 Park Ave. S., New York, NY 10016. 212-MU3-8960. (www.dramatists.com) who also handle performance rights.

THE LADY WITH ALL THE ANSWERS. © 2006 by David Rambo. Reprinted by permission of Mary Harden, Harden-Curtis Assoc., 850 7th Ave. #903, New York, NY 10019. The entire text has been published by Dramatists Play Service, 440 Park Ave. S., New York, NY 10016. 212-MU3-8960. (www.dramatists.com) who also handle performance rights.

LARRY AND THE WEREWOLF. ©2006 by Jeff Goode. Reprinted by permission of the author. The entire text has been published by Broadway Play Publishing, Inc., 56 E. 81st St., New York, NY 10028-8358. 212-772-8334 (www.broadwayplaypubl.com). who also handle performance rights.

LA TEMPESTAD. © 2005 by Larry Loebell. Reprinted by permission of the author. The entire text has been published by NY Theatre Experience in Playing with Canons. (www.nyte.org) For performance rights, contact Elaine Devlin Literary, c/o Plus Entertainment, 20 W. 23rd St. 3rd. Fl, New York, NY 10010.

LOOKING. © 2006 by Norm Foster. Reprinted by permission of Samuel French, Inc., 45 W. 25th St., New York, NY 10010. 212-206-8990 (www.samuelfrench.com) who also handle performance rights. The entire text has been published by Samuel French, Inc.

MADAGASCAR. © 2006 by J. T. Rogers. Reprinted by permission of John Buzzetti, The Gersh Agency, 41 Madison Ave., New York, NY 10010. The entire text has been published by Dramatists Play Service, 440 Park Ave. S., New York, NY 10016. 212-MU3-8960 (www.dramatists.com), who also handle performance rights.

MAIDEN'S PROGENY. © 2006 by Le Wilhelm. Reprinted by permission of Samuel French, Inc., 45 W. 25th St., New York, NY 10010. 212-206-8990 (www.samuelfrench.com) who also handle performance rights. The entire text has been published by Samuel French, Inc.

MAKE ME A MATCH. © 2006 by Lawrence Roman. Reprinted by permission of Samuel French, Inc., 45 W. 25th St., New York, NY 10010. 212-206-8990. (www.samuelfrench.com) who also handle performance rights. The entire text has been published by Samuel French, Inc.

A MOTHER, A DAUGHTER AND A GUN. ©2006 by Barra Grant. Reprinted by permission of Peter Hagan, The Gersh Agency, 41 Madison Ave., New York, NY 10010. The entire text has been published by Samuel French, Inc., 45 W. 25th St., New York, NY 10010. 212-306-8990 (www.samuelfrench.com), who also handle performance rights.

A MOTHER'S LOVE. © 2006 by Craig Pospisil. Reprinted by permission of Patricia McLaughlin, Beacon Artists Agency. 120 E. 56th St. #540, New York 10022, The entire text has been published (as part of *Life Is Short*) by Dramatists Play Service, 440 Park Ave. S., New York, NY 10016. 212-MU3-8960. (www.dramatists.com), who also handle performance rights.

MY DEAH. © 2004 by John Epperson. Reprinted by permission of the author. The entire text has been published in an acting edition by Samuel French, Inc., 45 W. 25th St., New York, NY 10010. 212-206-8990 (www.samuelfrench.com). who also handle performance rights.

'NAMI. © 2006 by Chad Beckim. Reprinted by permission of the author. The entire text has been published by New York Theatre Experience in *Plays and Playwrights 2007* (www.nyte.org). For performance rights contact the author at: chadbeckim1@yahoo.com

OFFICE SONATA. © 2005 by Andy Chmelko. Reprinted by permission of Josh Sherman, Sixth and Park Management, 600 Park Ave. #1, Hoboken, NJ 07030. The entire text has been published by New York Theatre Experience in *Plays and Playwrights 2007* (www.nyte.org). For performance rights contact Sixth and Park Management.

OVER THE TAVERN. © 2006 by Tom Dudzick. All rights reserved. Reprinted by permission of Playscripts, Inc. To purchase acting editions of this play, or to obtain stock or amateur perfor-